T0313614

THE UNIVERSITY OF MICHIGAN

CENTER FOR SOUTH AND SOUTHEAST ASIAN STUDIES

MICHIGAN PAPERS ON SOUTH AND SOUTHEAST ASIA

Ann Arbor, Michigan

LAW AND KINGSHIP IN THAILAND

DURING THE REIGN OF KING CHULALONGKORN

by

David M. Engel

Ann Arbor

Center for South and Southeast Asian Studies
The University of Michigan
1975

Michigan Papers on South and Southeast Asia, 9

Open access edition funded by the National Endowment for the Humanities/
Andrew W. Mellon Foundation Humanities Open Book Program.

Library of Congress Catalog Card Number 74-20343
International Standard Book No. 0-89148-009-9

Printed and bound by CPI Group (UK) Ltd, Croydon, CR0 4YY

ISBN 978-0-89148-009-9 (paper)
ISBN 978-0-472-12798-6 (ebook)
ISBN 978-0-472-90194-4 (open access)

For Jaruwan

CONTENTS

Acknowledgements   ix

Chapter 1: Changing Theories of Royal Authority, Law
and Government   1

A. Theories of Law and Kingship   1

B. Changes in the Administrative Structure   20

Notes   27

Chapter 2: The Legislative Function   33

A. The Early Period: Privy Council and Council
of State   33

B. The Later Period: The Legislative Council,
Provincial Legislative Powers, and the
Legislative Function During the Regency   43

1. The Legislative Council   43

2. Provincial Legislative Powers and the
Legislative Function During the Regency   49

3. Comparisons with the Parliamentary
System   53

Notes   57

Chapter 3: The Judicial Function   59

A. Transformation of the Judiciary   59

1. Historical Perspective   60

2. Structural Reorganization of the Judiciary
under King Chulalongkorn   63

a. The Early Period   63

b. The Ministry of Justice and the
Bangkok Courts   66

c. The Ministry of Justice and the
Provincial Courts   69

3. New Laws and Procedures for the Thai
   Judiciary   74

B. Implications of the Change   77

  1. Unification and Extension of the
     Centralized Judiciary   77

  2. The Distinction between Civil and
     Criminal Law   79

  3. Appeals   82

  4. Exercise of the Judicial Powers of the
     King   85

  Notes   91

Chapter 4: Rights of Private Citizens   95

A. Social Legislation   95

B. Suits Against Government Officials   100

C. The Right to Fair Treatment by the
   Judicial and Penal System   103

D. Rights of Speech   110

E. The Right to Representation in Government   113

  Notes   116

Chapter 5: Conclusion   119

  Notes   125

Bibliography   127

ACKNOWLEDGMENTS

This study of the changes in Thai law and kingship during the reign of King Chulalongkorn originated largely as a result of the encouragement and guidance of Professor David Joel Steinberg, formerly on the History faculty at the University of Michigan and now Assistant to the President of Brandeis University. Professor Steinberg urged me to bring together my study of law and Thai history in a description of the transformation of Thailand during the late nineteenth and early twentieth centuries as seen from a legal point of view. With his assistance, and the assistance of others, I undertook to write an essay based for the most part upon those royal enactments from 1873 to 1910 which seemed to me most crucially to affect the executive, legislative, and judicial functions of the king and the rights of private citizens. An earlier draft of this study served as my master's thesis in South and Southeast Asian Studies at the University of Michigan.

I am deeply indebted to the late Paul G. Kauper, Henry M. Butzel Professor of Law at the University of Michigan, who shared with Professor Steinberg the task of supervising this project from its inception. I feel very fortunate to have had throughout my research the benefit of Professor Kauper's insights and broad understanding of comparative constitutional systems. Like so many other people who studied under him, I shall always value the memory of his wisdom, his dignity, and his great kindness.

Ajaan Nidhi Aeusrivongse, my instructor and friend, was enormously helpful to me in reading and analyzing the Thai texts and placing them in proper historical perspective. Ajaan Nidhi, who is a member of the History faculty at Chiengmai University, generously gave many hours of his time to discuss these matters with me. Although my conclusions may not necessarily be the same as his in each instance, it is impossible for me to imagine what shape this study would have taken without his suggestions, his criticisms, and his creative insights into the history of the period.

Professor David K. Wyatt of Cornell University provided me with valuable assistance at the beginning of my research, by recommending and helping me to obtain certain important books and documents. Professor Wyatt later read and helped me to revise the completed manuscript as well.

Professor John K. Whitmore of the History Department at the University of Michigan gave me a great deal of help in revising the earlier draft of my study. Under his supervision I rewrote much of the material dealing with the period before King Chulalongkorn's reign.

I am also grateful to Professor Alton L. Becker, Director of the Center for South and Southeast Asian Studies at the University of Michigan, for reading and helping to arrange for the publication of this essay. Both Professor Becker and Professor L.A. Peter Gosling, the previous Director of the Center, encouraged and assisted me throughout my joint program of law and area studies. Mr. John Musgrave, Southeast Asian Bibliographer at the University of Michigan, was very generous in helping me to obtain certain materials which I used in this project and in reading and criticizing the completed manuscript. Mrs. Jennifer Broomfield endured my last-minute changes without complaint and typed the entire essay for publication.

My parents throughout this period, as always, were a source of warm support and encouragement. It has been a special pleasure to me that they have shared my fascination with Thailand during the past years and have made it the subject of their own interests and explorations.

My wife, to whom this essay is dedicated, was its first cause and its final editor. More than she may realize, this study owes its existence to her.

CHAPTER 1

CHANGING THEORIES OF ROYAL AUTHORITY, LAW, AND GOVERNMENT

A. Theories of Law and Kingship

Until the era of King Rama V, the Thai conceptions of law and of kingship were interrelated to an extraordinary degree. The predominant position of the king as creature, creator, and protector of the legal system was a concept which persisted into the middle of King Chulalongkorn's reign when it, like many other traditional assumptions, was challenged and to some extent reshaped by revisionist thought. Despite the broad sweep of reform under King Chulalongkorn, however, many of the traditional ideas and practices were retained. If any monarch wielded absolute power or played the ancient role of paternalistic and benevolent ruler, surely it was King Chulalongkorn at the height of his reign. And yet, during this very apotheosis of absolute rule, ideas crept in, were tolerated, were even encouraged and promoted by the ruler himself, which challenged the centrality of the king to the Thai legal system. In a curious way, the very transformation of Thai law which measured the height of absolute power also marked the beginning of a separation of the two concepts of law and kingship, a process which would ultimately lead to the termination of the absolute monarchy in June 1932.

The unusual historical predominance of the traditional Thai king, both legally and politically, derived not from a single conception of law and kingship, but from a synthesis of several different and sometimes contradictory conceptions which entered Thai society over the course of several centuries. Perhaps the earliest form of kingship was the patriarchal monarchy of which there is evidence dating from the kingdom of Sukhothai in the thirteenth and fourteenth centuries. This earlier theory was cast in familial terms, with the monarch

1

ruling his small but independent kingdom like a wise and
benevolent father. The king was not yet the distant, semi-
divine figure which he was to become. In theory and in
legend he was accessible to the people and ready to aid in the
settlement of disputes among members of his "family":

> In the gateway of the palace a bell is hung;
> if anyone in the kingdom has some grievance
> or some matter that is ulcerating his entrails
> and troubling his mind, and wishes to lay it
> before the king, the way is easy: he has
> only to strike the bell hung there. Every
> time King Rama Khamheng hears this appeal, he
> interrogates the plaintiff about the matter
> and gives an entirely impartial decision. [1]

Subsequent conceptions of Thai kingship were more
explicitly Indian in origin, entering Thai society by way of
the Khmer empire on the one hand and the Mon people on the
other. The Khmer influence, increasingly apparent in the
development of the kingdom of Ayutthaya, made of the king a
more distant and stern figure, identified in theory with the
Hindu gods Shiva and Vishnu, surrounded therefore with Hindu
ritual, advised in the mysteries of the sacred law by his own
Brahmin legal experts, and bearing towards the people the
relationship of master to servant rather than father to
child. [2] This was the concept of king as Devarāja, the awe-
inspiring and god-like figure who so impressed European
visitors to the Thai court in the seventeenth century. [3] This
form of kingship led to the characterization of the Thai
monarch as čhao chiwit, or "Lord of Life," with a theoretically
absolute power of life and death over his subjects.

The stern and forbidding image of the king as Devarāja
mingled to some extent with Buddhist conceptions of kingship
which came to Thai society through the influence of the Mons.
The Mon people of southern Thailand and Burma, strongly
influenced by Theravada Buddhism, had transformed many of the
Hindu precepts of law and kingship into a less forbidding theory
of royal authority. [4] It was probably from them that the Thai
concept of king as idealized ruler was drawn. According to
this theory the king was to promote the teachings of the Buddha
and to conform his own behavior to the ethical principles which

the Buddha had articulated. The Devarāja conception in
Thailand was thus reformulated in a most significant way
during the Ayutthaya period:

> The Brahmanical concept of the Devarāja, the
> king as god, was modified to make the king the
> embodiment of the Law, while the reign of
> Buddhist moral principles ensured that he
> should be measured against the Law. The effect
> of this transformation was to strengthen the
> checks which, in the Khmer empire, Brahmans
> had attempted to exercise against despotic
> excesses of absolute rule. [5]

Central to the king's function as upholder of the sacred
law was the Thai thammasat, a form of legal code derived from
the Hindu dharma-śāstras as restated by Mon legal specialists.
The thammasat set forth the history of the world and man, the
evolution of laws, and the origin of kings. It defined the
relationship between the individual and the state and prescribed
the norms by which the ruler should be governed in his actions.
It contained legal precepts by which the relations between
people were to be regulated, together with certain inter-
pretations which those precepts had inspired through the years.
The thammasat was, in short, the fundamental statement of
royal law and legitimacy in traditional Thailand.

The centrality of the thammasat to the Thai system of
law and kingship was reaffirmed by King Chulalongkorn's
ancestor, the founder of the Čhakkri dynasty. In the first
years of the Bangkok period the law of the previous Ayutthaya
period had been used in the new capital. It is said, however,
that King Rama I ordered a thorough revision and purification
of this traditional body of law after a famous lawsuit came
before him in 1804 on a petition for his final judgement. A
woman known as Amdaeng Pǫm sought to divorce her husband,
Nai Bunsri, who resisted her suit and alleged on appeal that
she herself had been guilty of adultery with one of the judges.
King Rama I determined that the divorce had properly been
granted under the law as it then existed, but he believed it
unfair to allow a woman to obtain a favorable decree whenever
she requested a divorce, without any inquiry into allegations of
misconduct on her part. [6] Believing that the provision requiring

such a result was symptomatic of a number of defects and inequities which had crept into the legal system over the years, Rama I established a Royal Commission to examine and revise the entire corpus of Thai law. The result of their efforts, completed in 1805, was known as the Law of the Three Seals, representing in the eyes of its creators a return to the purity of the thammasat itself. [7]

The Thai thammasat, as restated in the Law of the Three Seals, elaborated considerably upon the format of the Manu dharma-śāstra, the Hindu code from which it was indirectly derived. Although the traditional Indian texts contained eighteen law titles concerning litigation, the Thai version consisted of 39 such chapters, or laksana. Among the subjects of the different laksana were, for example, laksana rap fong, the law for receiving plaints, laksana phua mia, the law of husband and wife, laksana that, the law of slavery, and laksana phayan, the law of evidence. Ten of the laksana dealt with procedural matters, while the remaining 29 concerned topics of substantive law. [8]

The Thai thammasat also differed from the Hindu śāstras in that it reflected the strong influence of Buddhist philosophy and cosmogony. The Hindu Code of Manu was the word of Brahmā himself, creator of the world, as it had been transmitted to his offspring, the legendary Manu, and then to ten Sages who preserved the teachings for mankind. [9] In the Thai-Mon version, on the other hand, Manu was a counselor to the first monarch in the history of the world. King Mahāsammata, a Bodhisattva, had been elected to rule by primitive men when they found it necessary to choose a leader from among themselves in order to settle their disputes. The king could interpret but not create the law, and it was Manu's role to be raised into the heavens until he reached the wall surrounding the world. On this wall were carved the sacred laws which Manu read and recounted to King Mahāsammata. These laws became, in the Thai version, the foundation of the thammasat. [10]

Whereas Hindu theory would emphasize the divine foundation of the rule of kings, the Thai thammasat described a King of Righteousness, a Great Elect, who followed certain precepts of just rule and abided by the ten kingly virtues: alms-

giving, morality, liberality, rectitude, gentleness, self-
restriction, non-anger, non-violence, forbearance, and
non-obstruction. [11] The king was to study the thammasat with
care and observe the four principles of justice: to examine
the propriety and quality of all work performed for him; to
protect and promote those who were honest; to obtain royal
revenues by just means alone; to maintain the happiness and
prosperity of his kingdom. [12] The king was not divine, but if
he ruled according to the principles of righteousness he could
become recognized as a čhakkraphat (chakravartin), a Universal
Sovereign possessing great power and moral influence throughout the world. [13]

In theory, therefore, the thammasat should have served
as a limit upon the exercise of absolute power by the Thai
kings. Although the king could not be restrained by any law
of man, his power was subject to the moral authority of the
thammasat itself, and he was bound to observe the rules and
precepts contained in it. In fact, however, there was no
formally constituted class or group in Thai society which
could enforce these rules against the king. The Devarāja
concept of kingship, with its air of mystery, aloofness, and
ritual, together with the Theravada Buddhist concept of the
king as an embryonic Buddha, combined to create a theory of
kingship which could indeed lend substance to claims of
unchallengeable and absolute power. [14]

Regardless of the temporal power which a Thai king
might wield, however, he was subject like any other being to
the workings of thamma, or dharma, a concept basic to
the philosophy of the thammasat. It was believed that certain
immutable rules operated in the moral universe just as the
laws of physics operate in the natural universe. These
inexorable rules of moral behavior existed above the sometimes
arbitrary actions of individuals or their rulers, meting out
rewards and punishments in a transcendental system of justice.
The workings of thamma were the essence of the sacred laws
which Manu had learned and passed on to mankind. The concept
of thamma, or dharma, has been explained in the following
terms by a leading western historian of Indian and Thai law:

> In external terms, dharma is the action which,
> provided it is conformable to the order of things,

permits man to realise his destiny to the full,
sustains him in this life, and assures his well-
being after death. By its own virtue that act
produces a spiritual benefit for him who has
performed it, which will necessarily bear fruit
in the other world. Conversely, an act contrary
to dharma, called adharma, necessarily involves
a sanction, a "fall" for the one who does it, which
will strike him in his future existence if not
actually in his present life. "Destroyed, Dharma
destroys; protected, he protects": so says Manu
(VIII. 15). In internal terms, dharma signifies
the obligation, binding upon every man who desires
that his actions should bear fruit, to submit
himself to the laws which govern the universe and
to direct his life in consequence. That obligation
constitutes his duty: and that is a further sense
of the word. [15]

The principle of thamma, or dharma, provides one
explanation for the limited capacity of the traditional Thai
monarch to create permanent laws. [16] The king had no
theoretical power to legislate but merely to issue commands
which would protect the people and preserve the principles of
the thammasat. As chief judge, the Thai king could also
declare the law when disputes of the people came to him on
petition. In theory, however, these edicts and judicial
decisions had no permanent force. They were always subject
to revision or reversal by later rulers. The collection of
king-made law was known as rachasat, in contrast to the
thammasat itself. Rachasat was for the most part temporary
law, binding on the people because of the power of the king,
but lacking the inviolability and permanence of the thammasat.
Conceivably a king could, by royal edict, oppose the very
essence of the thammasat, but such deviations and impurities,
it was believed, would not last long. A later monarch, like
Rama I in his revision of the legal corpus, would inevitably
restore the law to its proper and permanent form. Such
restorations were inevitable because of the inexorable workings
of the thamma which would sooner or later destroy all unjust
laws:

Commands of kings can only endure if they are in

conformity with Dharma, and not because of the
absolute power of kings, but because of the
transcending nature of the rule of dharma which is
underlying them. Rulers are auxiliaries of Dharma.
The true law-givers are Manu and those inspired
Sages who have revealed Dharma once for all. [17]

Despite the theoretical inability of traditional Thai kings
to enact permanent laws, it has been observed that certain
royal decrees did in fact attain the status of legislation which
was preserved as part of the sacred code. The Thai thammasat
records not only the fundamental precepts attributed to Manu
(known as munla-at, or mula-attha) but also those rules of
law which were outgrowths (sakha-at, or sakha-attha) of the
fundamental precepts. These outgrowths came into existence
as Thai kings interpreted and elaborated the sacred law.
The decrees were strictly speaking rachasat, yet they could
acquire a permanent and respected status if they conformed
sufficiently to the sacred law. By a formal process, royal
enactments could be incorporated into the very text of the
thammasat:

A procedure is expressly provided for the
transformation of a royal decision into a rule
of law. They must be stripped of the features
which gave rise to them, and reduced in abstract
terms to the concise form of the precepts of the
law. They could then be added to the text of the
dhammasattha itself under the relevant rubric. [18]

The remarkable legislative activity of King Chulalongkorn was
perhaps anticipated by this embryonic law-making capacity of the
traditional Thai kings. [19] In so far as the royal decisions and
decrees were themselves thamma, they could be abstracted
and integrated into the corpus of Thai law. In so far as the
laws departed from thamma, they became a nullity when the power
of their creator ended.

This distinction between temporary and lasting laws may
reflect what one anthropologist has described as a fundamental
dualism in the Thai social order. On the one hand there is
"merit" which is gained through selfless acts, particularly
acts by rich or powerful men such as kings. Such meritorious

acts are characterized by their effectiveness and their
permanence. On the other hand, there is "power," which
may also lead to short-term success but which, because of
its amoral character, will lack the permanence of truly
meritorious acts. The products of power, without the
presence of merit, will in time be destroyed. [20] This
analysis applies as well to the enactments of the Thai kings.
By virtue of their extraordinary power, the kings could
command almost any short-term result they might wish,
but unless their edicts were supported by selfless and
meritorious purposes, as delineated in the thammasat,
they would not least. Despite the opportunity for arbitrary
and capricious behavior there was thus a certain stability
and justice in the traditional system of rule:

> Though power blurs the clear edges of cosmic
> justice, one may think of justice lagging
> behind, like a court with a clogged calendar,
> in exacting punishments and awarding
> compensations. [21]

It is clear, however, that in the short run the power
of the king was supreme to preserve the law, to interpret
the law, and to create new law. There was no Parliament
free to act as a legislative counterbalance. There was
no tradition of a strong and independent judiciary which
might create a system of common law. There was no Magna
Carta standing between king and subjects as a symbol of
the rights and liberties of individuals which could be
enforced against an unjust king. In short, the essence of
the law was the king himself. The law was a justification
of kingship, and the king was the interpreter and creator
of law, limited only by the moral constraints enumerated
in the thammasat and by the belief that the rules of thamma
would eventually work their retribution upon unjust acts.

This, then, was the tradition of law and kingship
which was challenged and to some extent changed during the
era of reforms over which King Chulalongkorn presided.
As political pressures from the colonial powers on Thailand's
borders became more intense, as western ideas of government
came increasingly to influence the Thai elite, the traditional
assumptions were called more and more into question. King

Chulalongkorn's father, King Mongkut, had already found
it necessary to exercise his legislative powers more actively
than had his predecessors. There was a suggestion of new
thoughts about royal legitimacy as well in King Mongkut's
revision of the traditional ceremony of allegiance to the
king. Instead of accepting passively a unilateral pledge
of loyalty from his officials and court, King Mongkut
made the ceremony bilateral by offering his own pledge as
sovereign to be loyal to his subjects. [22] Hints of change,
of new theories and ideas, were in the air. Significantly,
these ideas reached the king and the elite before they reached
the people. For this reason it was possible for the king to
seize the initiative, to act decisively not only to forestall
colonial intervention but to prevent public disenchantment
with the traditional system of absolute rule. [23]

An essay by Prince Phitchit Prichakǫn entitled "A
Consideration of Justice [thammasan winitchai]" written
in 1885,exemplifies the transition from traditional Thai and
Indian legal theory to newer ideas which were often influenced
by western thought. [24] Prince Phitchit was a brother of King
Chulalongkorn and served as a member of his Privy Council
and later as Minister of Justice. Unlike many princes of his
and later generations, however, he was not sent to Europe
for his education. For this reason, perhaps, his ideas of
justice were more strongly rooted in the traditional than
was true in the case of his brothers and nephews. Nevertheless,
his essay was a conscious attempt to formulate a system of
natural law, implying some form of social compact between
the modern king and his subjects based upon the ancient concept
of thamma.

Prince Phitchit in his essay observed that "thamma"
was linked to the Thai word "thamniam ," which meant custom
or tradition. It was from thamniam, or custom, that a
system of law was formed. To be precise, there were four
thamma which acted as a foundation for the social activities
of all people and which served as a basis for their well-being
and contentment. The king, therefore, could enact laws
based upon these four thamma in order to ensure their
protection within the kingdom and thereby provide for the
welfare of his people. The four thamma to which Prince

Phitchit referred were:

(1)   The providing of food and sustenance. The king could enact any law which would assure adequate food and clothing for his people.

(2)   The creation of plenty or abundance. The king could enact laws which provided for times of war or famine when men could not produce food for themselves.

(3)   Equality and fair treatment. In men's necessary dealings with one another, particularly in the area of trade and commerce, laws should protect against the taking of unfair advantage.

(4)   Peacefulness and protection from danger. The king could protect his people by means of military strength from dangers both external and internal.

The power of the king to create law, according to this scheme, would seem to arise out of four basic rules of nature which were made apparent through ancient social customs and usage. This theory alone represented a considerable shift from the broad power of the absolute monarch to enact any law necessary to protect the vague and generalized precepts of the thammasat. In addition, Prince Phitchit's treatment stressed to an unusual degree the role of the common people both as beneficiaries of all proper laws and as source of the legal system itself, for it was by their customary practices that the four thamma were revealed.

Prince Phitchit observed that the four thamma were constantly threatened with destruction by the four evils or prejudices: illicit desires, hatred or anger, fear, and ignorance. The role of the king was to protect the four thamma from transgressions, both direct and indirect, through the rewards and punishments which he meted out. By articulating and publicizing a fair system of law and justice, the king made known to all his subjects their rights and duties towards one another. He thereby constructed a permanent framework for the settlement of disputes and a body of rules for the conduct of the people's affairs.

The concept of king as chao chiwit, or Lord of Life, was conspicuously absent from Prince Phitchit's analysis. This was no monarch with absolute and arbitrary power of

life and death over his helpless subjects. Rather, the
king was a figure who performed certain socially necessary
tasks, whose legislative powers were defined by the basic
needs of the people, whose system of law arose not from
any sacred and mysterious source but from the nature and
practices of men as social beings. Traditional Buddhist
thought was central to Prince Phitchit's analysis, but it
served less to idealize the king as a future Buddha than to
explain the necessity of fair laws for the protection of
property and the public well-being.

Prince Phitchit Prichakọn, in his essay on justice,
was a transitional figure. He was a member of the traditional
elite dealing in an imaginative way with influential and
alien ideas about the legitimacy of government under law.
A more dramatic and historically significant document was
written only two years later by a group of eleven princes
and officials all of whom, unlike Prince Phitchit, had
travelled or studied abroad. Among these men were three of
King Chulalongkorn's brothers: Prince Phitthayalap, Prince
Naret, and Prince Sawat, the last having just completed his
legal studies at Oxford. [25] The document, presented to the
king on January 8, 1887, was a petition proposing bluntly
that the present form of government be replaced by a
parliamentary system under a written constitution. [26]

The petition came near the end of a long period of
quiet after the young king's initial flurry of reform, and
was remarkable for several reasons. The very fact of its
presentation to the king revealed the extent to which ideas
of governmental change were current among the elite and
tolerated by the monarch himself. The mildness of the king's
reply was further evidence of his readiness to listen even
to ideas which might challenge the very legitimacy of his
rule. The petition also underlined the extremity of the
danger to Thailand's security, threatened on both sides
by the aggressive colonialist activities of England and
France, and feared by the petitioners and the king to the
extent that they were willing to consider radical internal
changes.

The petition opened with the frank statement that

Thailand, as a country of little real power, was seriously threatened by countries of great power. Thailand, it was argued, should follow Japan's example and thoroughly Europeanize her government in order to protect against this threat. The European countries, despite their aggressive intentions, would not seize a weaker nation without some pretext to justify their warlike act:

(1)   the pretext of humanitarianism--the invader would assert that its aim was to bring happiness and advancement to all men equally;

(2)   the pretext that the backwardness of Asian countries could somehow hinder the European countries in their own advancement;

(3)   the pretext that certain ineffective Asian governments were incapable of protecting the persons and property of Europeans and other Asians within their borders, a situation which could be rectified by the replacement of the local government with a colonial administration;

(4)   the pretext of commerce--the European countries could assure their own development and prosperity by using the Asian countries as markets and as sources of valuable raw materials. The petitioners compared the logic of the Europeans to a familiar rule of Thai law: when a person who owned a rice field failed to put it to productive use, an outsider might be permitted to take over the field in the hope that he would prove more worthy of possession.

The petitioners criticised on a number of grounds the moderate reforms already begun by the king. Their criticisms may be grouped under three general headings: (1) A gradualist approach to reform would inevitably fail as a defense against foreign encroachments. Thailand could not merely adopt certain aspects of western advancement without making fundamental changes in her system of government. The gradualist approach had been tried in Japan and had failed. Superficial reforms, like the abolition of slavery or the establishment of a modern telegraph and postal system were inadequate to inspire respect among the European countries, and their sympathy or pity alone would not protect Thailand. (2) Thailand could no longer rely on her foreign trade or her natural resources as an inducement for amicable relations with the colonial powers. If anything,

these factors would tempt the Europeans to seize Thailand
rather than to respect her sovereignty. Existing treaties
were likewise of little use, as the example of China clearly
proved. Nor should Thailand feel secure in her geographical
position as a buffer zone between the English and French
colonies, for these countries would still try to seize as much
territory and special advantage as possible. (3) Finally,
Thailand could not depend upon the protection of international
law as a deterrent against aggressive actions by the European
powers. This law was intended to apply only to the "civilized"
nations of the world and would surely fail if invoked by a
country like Thailand against a country like England or France.
Japan's rights as an equal and independent nation under international law had been recognized only after her government
was completely transformed and westernized, and the same
would be true in the case of Thailand.

What was proposed, then, was a European style of
government. The present system was seen as too heavily
dependent upon the king and royalty for its effective
functioning. Moreover, it was believed among Europeans
that the chief ministers did not work for the good of their
ministries and should be held more directly accountable to
the wishes of the people. The petitioners did not give many
details of the new system they wished to see installed, but
the proposal in its outline form was sweeping indeed. A
constitution was to be promulgated and a parliament established. The absolute monarchy would be replaced by a
constitutional monarchy in which the king could share many
of his present responsibilities rather than personally involving
himself with each item of government work. A cabinet would
be established with major decision-making powers. Corruption
would be ended and government salaries raised to a sufficient
level. There would be equal rights under law for all persons,
including equality in the methods of taxation; and the laws
generally would grant equal status to Thais and westerners.
Old laws and customs would be eliminated if they offended
Europeans or impeded progress. Freedom of speech would be
guaranteed, including the right of public meetings and a free
press.

Despite some fairly substantial difficulties anticipated
in the implementation of these drastic changes, the writers

argued that the transformation could be successfully accom -
plished. Moreover the Thai people, far from being dismayed
by the loss of their traditional institutions of government,
would feel even greater love and allegiance for their country
when they realized that their rights under law were the equal
of any people's on earth.

King Chulalongkorn, in his written reply, firmly
declined to follow the suggestions of the petitioners. [27] He
cautioned that changes which might appear to them to be
warranted by the threat of foreign intervention would nevertheless be strongly opposed by certain groups within the Thai
government. These groups were in a position to limit the
extent and success of any reforms which the king might wish
to undertake. Although the king agreed with many of the
criticisms set forth in the petition, he was unable to conclude
that an immediate westernization of the government would
produce beneficial results.

King Chulalongkorn assured the petitioners that he had
no personal or selfish interest in preserving the absolute
power of the Thai monarchy. At the beginning of his reign,
he reminded them, he had been a mere puppet while the regent
had assumed all real power. The king compared his situation
during those years to that of a child who, in flying a kite,
had let out all the string. The child was forced to exert his
utmost strength merely to keep his balance or to prevent the
kite from escaping. Little by little he had rewound the string.
Since the powerful regent and his ministers had neglected the
traditional legislative function, the young king had seized
upon this area to reassert his royal power. He and his
advisory council through the enactment of new laws became,
as King Chulalongkorn described it, a kind of opposition to
the established government. As time went on the king had
gradually recovered control over the executive function as
well. While his executive powers increased, however, the
legislative function fell into disuse, for the king was unable
to manage both areas effectively at the same time. The affairs
of modern government had become too complex, and the king
lacked able assistants. In the interest of strengthening his
position as chief executive, the king had been forced to
sacrifice the vitality of the Thai law-making function.

Despite the weakened condition of the legislative function, however, King Chulalongkorn cited two factors which prevented him from establishing a parliamentary form of government in Thailand at that time. The first factor was the inefficiency of the Thai bureaucracy, which had to be reformed and made more effective before any broad political change could be attempted. The second factor was that Thailand then lacked a sufficient number of trained men who could participate successfully in the drafting of new laws. Furthermore, it was certain that the powerful ministers would resist all such changes and, if it developed that they were incompetent to perform their new duties, might even resign in large numbers, creating an unprecedented crisis in the Thai political system. In short, the king was able to assure the petitioners only that change was inevitably drawing nearer, that reform of the administrative system was the necessary first step, and that such changes as they themselves advocated could come only after the initial reforms were successfully achieved.

From this dramatic confrontation between the reforming king and an element of his western-educated elite, there emerged a sharpened picture of the challenge facing the traditional system. Without doubt, the time was one of great peril to Thailand's sovereignty. Nor did many of the new leaders of King Chulalongkorn's generation believe the present system of government to be capable of meeting the dangers their country faced. Change was inevitable if colonization was to be avoided, but the question was what kind of change and how fast and by what means. The king was either unwilling or unable to sacrifice the traditional system of law and kingship for an entirely new system based upon a constitution and a parliament. But he was also unwilling and unable to permit the present situation to continue without fundamental reform.

King Chulalongkorn's own theories of law and kingship had begun to emerge and develop from the very first days of his reign as king. Although he was placed upon the throne in 1868 at the age of fifteen, the actual task of governing was officially performed by a regent until King Chulalongkorn's second coronation as an adult in 1873. On the latter occasion,

the king issued a well-known proclamation abolishing the
ancient custom of prostration before royalty and high officials.
In this symbolic enactment are found the first indications of
a new attitude toward progress, reform, and kingship.

The young king in his proclamation described the
practice of prostration as a symbol of oppression imposed
by those of great status and power. This in itself was a
social evil, for it brought misery and weariness to the
little men who had to crouch and crawl and prostrate
themselves before figures of greater importance. This concern
with the happiness and well-being of the common people was
characteristic of the benevolent paternalism which ran through
many of King Chulalongkorn's writings and decrees. The
proclamation also noted that wherever such oppressive
practices had been eliminated, prosperity and progress had
surely followed. This, too, was a pattern of thought which
would recur throughout the years. By adopting certain
practices of the prosperous and developed countries, it was
believed that Thailand could itself become prosperous and
developed. It was this very approach which the European-
educated petitioners criticized in their proposal for governmental change in 1887, referring to it as a superficial form
of gradualism. Finally, the young king concluded, the process
of change must be a gradual one. There would be many
changes, but they could not come all at once and must await
their appropriate time. For the present, it was sufficient
that by eliminating the custom of prostration the king had
called for an end to unjust oppression. 8 PKPS 114 . [28]

The process of change was indeed to prove a difficult
task, characterized by eager bursts of reforming zeal
followed by extended periods of political difficulty and inactivity. These peaks and valleys have been charted by one
historian as follows: an initial period of enthusiastic reform
lasted from 1873 until the "Front Palace Incident" of
December 1874. This crisis, involving an attempted coup by
the upparat or "second king," very nearly resulted in British
intervention against the throne, and was followed by more
than ten years of political caution and quiescence on the part
of King Chulalongkorn. A new period of activity began in the
second half of the 1880s, leading to the establishment of a

Cabinet system of government in 1892. Again, however, a
period of political crisis ensued and, in 1893, a conflict with
France nearly brought the two countries to war. For three
years, until 1895, the king rested and recovered both
politically and emotionally, but then began once again his task
of reform. It was during this period, from 1895 until the
king's death in 1910, that he permanently consolidated his
power, reorganized the government bureaucracy, reformed
the legal system, and twice travelled to Europe. [29]

Despite the varying pace of reform and governmental
change, however, a certain consistency and logical continuity
may be observed throughout the entire thirty-eight years of
King Chulalongkorn's reign. While change was encouraged
and promoted in many ways, it was resisted when it threatened
the structure of the monarchy itself. While European laws and
methods of government were studied and adopted to some extent,
the fundamental theory of constitutional government was held
at arm's length. While parliamentary forms and methods were
used in appointed legislative bodies, the notion of a truly
representative system never became more than a suggestion or
a prophecy.

The king himself in 1888 discussed the issue of royal
power and parliamentary government in a revealing passage
from his Speech Explaining the Governmental Reforms. [30]
The power of the king, he observed, was not specified by any
law for it was believed to be free from all restraints and
obstacles which could be imposed by law or man. However,
he continued, the actions of the king must always be fitting and
just, and for this reason he would not object to a delineation
of the powers of the king under law, as had been done in other
countries, when laws were established as a basis for government throughout the kingdom.

After making this rather remarkable concession,
however, the king digressed with the observation that such
limitations upon royal power had arisen in other countries
because of the people's dissatisfaction with an unrestrained
monarchy. This was not the case in Thailand, where the
people had requested no such limitation but the king himself
thought it should be imposed. King Chulalongkorn desired
such a change because, characteristically, he believed it

would advance and develop the country and bring happiness to the people. Since a different necessity compelled the specification of royal power in Thailand, the specification itself would take on a different form than it had in other countries. Thus, for example, Thailand could not be governed by a parliamentary system like those in certain European countries, nor would the people of Thailand desire such a system. Few men would be capable of serving as members of parliament and none would have experience in governing, so nothing would be accomplished. The people would not trust the members of parliament as they trusted the king, for they knew that the king was just and that he loved the people and desired their happiness more than any other person could.

Therefore, the king concluded, the royal power should be stated as it had always existed. Which is to say, the unlimited power of the king should be retained. While King Chulalongkorn suggested that the dramatic expression "Lord of Life" be abandoned, it was not because the Thai king lacked an absolute and unrestrained power to take the life of a subject without any cause. Rather it was because no king had ever done so, and presumably it would be inappropriate to publicize an arbitrary power which was never exercised.

In this fashion, King Chulalongkorn accepted the European concept of a royal power limited and specified by law and yet reaffirmed the traditional Thai concept of an absolute monarch capable of acting beyond the restraints of any temporal law. The apparent implication of this passage was that western forms would be studied, copied, and put to use in Thailand, but not beyond a certain point. The traditional Thai monarchy was so central to the society, to the people and to the effective functioning of the government, that the king would not permit it to be weakened or restrained by any law or rival institution.

In his reign as king, Rama V acted not to restrain the monarchy but to centralize and consolidate the royal power. In an article by two Thai scholars it is asserted that the key to this consolidation of power was the abolition of the phrai system-- a complex organization of master-client relationships through which the nobility had been able to control vast resources of manpower. By replacing the phrai hierarchy with a government-regulated system of taxation and military draft, the king weakened the political power of the nobility and was able to reform the old ministries and modernize the country's administrative structure without fear of opposition by the once powerful nobles. [31] However, these same writers contend, the king made no attempt to build political institutions which would preserve and protect the unprecedented power which he had accumulated. Indeed, it is argued that the king foresaw and desired the arrival of parliamentary government in Thailand at some point in the future. Although he did not consider a representative form of government possible during his own reign, it is contended that his ultimate purpose was to build the foundations for a democratic system. [32]

This matter has caused some disagreement among scholars. One Thai commentator, a confirmed anti-royalist, portrays King Chulalongkorn as a despot adamantly opposed to any form of true democracy:

> The urge underlying his efforts was to moder-
> nise his country. He went to Europe twice and
> brought back with him new ideas. But he was
> not unlike other despots, who can not extricate
> themselves from the lure of despotic power....
> (T)he King was sceptical as to the wisdom of a
> new order. The lure of absolute rule made
> him find all sorts of excuses to delay the change,
> even when that change was beating at the bars
> of circumstances.... It was a pity that
> democracy had no meaning to him at all, although
> in Europe it had reached its apogee. The King
> tried to evade it by a benevolent rule. [33]

A prominent English historian, on the other hand, saw King Chulalongkorn and his successors as "preparing the way for the adoption of a democratic form of government," [34] a view shared by many other observers both Thai and western.

This question is difficult indeed when framed in terms of motive or intent. The question may be recast, however, in terms which are more susceptible to analysis. It may be

asked what, precisely, was the legal effect of the various
acts and proclamations of King Chulalongkorn? To what
extent was there an alteration of or limitation upon the traditional royal power in relation to the law? How serious was
the experimentation with parliamentary forms of debate and
legislation? To what degree did the people gain a voice in
the workings of the government? What new rights were created
for the people under law, and how were these rights to be
enforced against the government?

A closer analysis of the laws enacted during the reign
of King Chulalongkorn will show that the answers to these
questions are not simple. In certain areas, the king showed
little willingness at all to depart from the traditional system.
The legislative function, for example, was firmly controlled
by the king throughout most of his reign. In other areas,
however, the situation was a good deal more complex. In the
area of individual rights, particularly, a change can be
observed which may foreshadow the revolutionary events that
followed the death of King Chulalongkorn by only twenty-two
years. After a brief description of the administrative reforms
under King Chulalongkorn, these questions will be examined
in some detail.

B.   Changes in the Administrative Structure

The reorganization of the government bureaucracy
was for King Chulalongkorn the reform upon which all further
progress depended. It was not the earliest of his important
reforms, coming as it did in the mid-1890s, but it was
fundamental to his reign in at least two respects. For one
thing, many of his other important changes, such as the
reorganization of the judiciary and the new laws of provincial
administration, can be understood only with reference to the
bureaucratic changes. Secondly, the transformation of the
bureaucracy provided a further expression of King Chulalongkorn's theory of kingship and revealed the extent to which he
was willing to depart from custom and tradition.

The traditional system of central administration was

itself the product of reform, an attempt by King Trailok of
Ayutthaya to transform a feudal style of territorial rule into
a "centralized and functionally differentiated system of
administration" under the personal direction of the king's
own ministers. [35] This effort, apparently influenced by
Khmer administrative concepts, became necessary as the
kingdom of Ayutthaya expanded geographically and required a
stronger and more effective method of centralized rule. With
the passage of time, however, the old bureaucracy lost much
of the "functionally differentiated" character which King
Trailok had sought to instill in it and became instead a confusing amalgam of territorial jurisdiction, overlapping responsibilities, and obsolete departments with little or no functional
justification.

The bureaucracy inherited by King Chulalongkorn was
led, at least in theory, by two principal figures: the Chief
Minister of mahatthai, the civilian division, and the Chief
Minister of kalahom, the military division. In addition, there
were four lesser ministries: khlang (the Treasury), müang
(the City), wang (the Palace), and na (Lands or Fields), and
a number of sub-ministries grouped under each of these. By
King Chulalongkorn's time, however, it was no longer accurate
to speak of the two greater and the four lesser ministries, nor
could most of the six ministries be described in terms of the
functions they were once intended to perform. It would be more
proper to group the khlang, or Treasury, with mahatthai and
kalahom as the most important of the ministries, and to
identify each of these three with a geographical region.

After a rebellion in the southern province of Nakorn
Sri Thammarat in 1691 A.D., it was thought desirable to
establish a more unified system of control over the manpower
and administration of the outlying areas. Kalahom therefore
assumed control over both civilian and military men available
for service in the South, while mahatthai performed a similar
function in the North. [36] In this way the distinction between
military and civilian administration was blurred, and the
geographical distinction replaced it once again in importance.
The primary function of both ministries became the registration
of manpower in their respective regions. [37] By the nineteenth
century this function was not only a means of asserting the

capital's control over the countryside, but was also a source of personal power, status, and wealth for the ministers and their subordinates. In addition to the registration of manpower, the Chief Ministers of mahatthai and kalahom administered the provinces under their respective controls, served as troop commanders to suppress revolts, established law courts within their ministries which heard appeals from the courts of the provincial governors, and collected taxes which were assessed within the provinces for use by the central government. [38]

The khlang, or Ministry of the Treasury, originally had charge of all revenues and expenses of the central government and, in its own courts of law, administered lawsuits arising from such matters. Another important function, the administration of foreign affairs, devolved upon a department within the khlang (the krom tha, or Department of the Port) as a result of its key role in regulating foreign trade. [39] In addition to these two major responsibilities, khlang at one time assumed control over the southern provinces which had until then been administered by kalahom. Overwhelmed by its numerous responsibilities, khlang abandoned its role as Treasurer for the central government, and this function was divided among the other departments of the bureaucracy. Later khlang's area of geographical control was to shrink to a limited number of coastal provinces, as kalahom resumed its supervision of the South. [40]

The other three ministries played lesser roles in the administration of the kingdom. Müang, also known as nakhǫnban, was in charge of police and other administrative affairs in the capital, as well as lawsuits involving serious offenses, and prisons. [41] Wang, dealt mostly with affairs concerning the palace itself, such as state ceremonies and personal requirements of the king and royal family. Na administered matters dealing with lands, rice crops, and the royal storehouses, as well as traditional agricultural ceremonies and other encouragements to the people to cultivate their crops with care and diligence. Like the other ministries, na had its own courts to decide cases arising within its area of responsibility, and also administered its own revenues and expenditures. [42]

The government in each province was modeled upon
the central government in the capital. The governor played a
role analogous to that of the king, while his deputy governor
was comparable to the upparat or "second king," and the
various local officials performed tasks similar to those of the
ministers. [43] The provinces outside the central region were
grouped into three classes, with those of higher rank exercising administrative control over those of lower rank. Although
the autonomy of the provinces tended to increase in proportion
to their distance from the capital, the king was able to exert
some direct control over local affairs by the appointment of
the governor and, through the Palace Ministry, the yokkrabat.
This latter figure was an inspector or "spy" for the central
government, empowered to make inquiries into all misbehavior of local officials including the governor himself, and
to sit with the governor in judging lawsuits, reporting at his
own discretion to the central government. [44]

To this brief outline of the traditional system of
administration, it should perhaps be added that two royal
councils served the king in rather different ways. The lukkhun
na sala was a group consisting of the ministers and the heads
of the important departments. They advised the king on
general matters of administration and on the issuance of
various royal enactments and communications with the
provinces. [45] The lukkhun na san luang, on the other hand,
was a group of Brahmin legal experts whose important and unusual role in deciding issues of law will be examined in Chapter
3. The reforms of King Chulalongkorn were to affect
significantly both of these royal councils.

King Chulalongkorn's criticism of the existing bureaucratic structure was sharp and specific. In his Speech Explaining the Governmental Reforms he observed that the traditional
framework of two chief ministries and four lesser ministries
bore little relationship to the present functional workings of
the government. A true analysis of the bureaucracy revealed
a senseless and anachronistic overlap between civilian and
military administrative institutions. [46] The judicial system,
scattered as it was among numerous ministries and departments, had become chaotic and unworkable. [47] The collecting
of taxes had likewise become hopelessly confused and corrupt,
with the resulting depletion of the royal treasuries leaving the

government paralyzed for lack of funds. [48]

In conclusion, the king contended that the old forms were no longer applicable to present needs. The effectiveness of each ministry depended largely on the particular man in charge, with the result that some ministries had little to do while others were overburdened with work. Hard work often went unrewarded, however, while lazy men reaped great benefits. Because the lines of administration had become so blurred and disorganized through the years, the king announced, it would be necessary to reform the entire bureaucracy. A new system would be established in which one person had over-all responsibility for each governmental function. In addition, accurate budgets would be prepared with expenditures appropriate to the work actually performed. [49]

The king went on to elaborate his plan to replace the old system of six ministries with a new system of twelve ministries, each with a specific function which the king expected it to perform. The six old divisions would be retained with important modifications:

(1) Mahatthai would now administer the northern provinces and Laos. [50]

(2) Kalahom would administer the southern, western, and eastern provinces and the Malayan territories. [51]

(3) Tha, formerly a section of the Treasury in charge of foreign affairs, would now control foreign affairs exclusively without any role in administering the coastal provinces as before.

(4) Wang would continue to supervise the affairs of the palace.

(5) Müang would be in charge of police, prisons, and the registration of citizens.

(6) Na would administer agriculture, commerce, forests, and mines.

In addition to the six old divisions, the king created six new ministries by splitting off some of the former functions of the traditional ministries, by elevating several sub-ministries to positions of greater importance, and by creating others out of whole cloth:

(7) Khlang, relieved of its numerous former responsibilities, would now devote its activities exclusively to

administering all revenues and expenditures for the entire government.

(8) Yutitham, a Ministry of Justice, would supervise all courts in the central system, hearing every type of case.

(9) Thammakan would administer religious affairs, schools, and hospitals.

(10) Yuthanathikan would perform the role of Defense Ministry and would handle all matters involving military conscription.

(11) Yothathikan would function as a Ministry of Public Works, in charge of building roads, canals, railroads, and telegraph and postal systems.

(12) Murathathikan would act as keeper of the privy seal and office of the royal clerks and scribes.[52]

In this manner, King Chulalongkorn first announced his sweeping revision of the traditional administrative structure. By 1896 the process of reorganization was largely completed and many of the older and more conservative ministers were replaced by the king's own appointees, often brothers of the king, men of the same generation and ideology, many with European educations. The administrative and political significance of this crucial change has been well documented.[53] In addition, however, King Chulalongkorn's transformation of the central administration also marked a significant departure from the traditional theories of kingship.

The reformation of the bureaucracy, like King Chulalongkorn's decree abolishing prostration, was evidence that the prupose of government was not merely to exist but to function, and to function in a way that would prove beneficial to the people. It was no longer sufficient that the government exist merely to maintain the monarch. King Chulalongkorn was determined to establish a rationalized and effective government in order to provide for the public well-being and thus ensure the longevity of the administration itself:

> We will administer the country well if we
> foster opportunities for the people to earn
> livings so that they are benefited by the
> government. Then they will pay the taxes
> which are the economic foundation of the
> government. Consequently, an effective

administration and a fostering of the ways
of providing for the livelihood of the people
are the most important, the final purposes
of the Kingdom. [54]

If, as it has been suggested, there was some "cosmo-
magic principle" underlying the ancient ministry structure, [55]
Rama V did not hesitate to disturb the heavens in his reformation of it. The traditional system was simply incapable of
acting in the manner which the king believed essential, not
only for the benefit of the people but for the preservation of
the kingdom. In his transformation of the administrative
system, moreover, King Chulalongkorn opened for himself a
gateway to the changes in law and society which he wished to
achieve. It was by this means alone that he could accomplish
his policies in the three general areas which are the primary
subjects of this study: the legislative function, the judicial
function, and the rights of private citizens.

NOTES

1.   G. Coedès, <u>The Making of South East Asia</u>, trans. from
     French by H.M. Wright (Berkeley, 1969), p. 145.
     This passage is from the well-known inscription by
     King Ram Khamhaeng of the Sukhothai period, 1292 A.D.
     A slightly less colorful translation of this passage, not
     differing significantly from the version I have chosen
     to quote, may be found in the recent detailed study by
     A.B. Griswold and Prasert ṇa Nagara, "The Inscrip-
     tion of King Rāma Gaṃhèn of Sukhodaya (1292 A.D.):
     Epigraphical and Historical Studies No. 9," <u>Siam
     Society Journal</u>, 59, pt.2 (1971), pp. 179-228.

2.   H.G. Quaritch Wales, <u>Ancient Siamese Government
     and Administration</u> (New York, 1965), p.16. Akin
     Rabibhadana, <u>The Organization of Thai Society in the
     Early Bangkok Period, 1782-1873</u> (Ithaca, 1969), p.40.

3.   Jeremy Kemp, <u>Aspects of Siamese Kingship in the
     Seventeenth Century</u> (Bangkok, 1969), p.8.

4.   Robert Lingat, <u>The Classical Law of India</u>, trans. from
     French with additions by J. Duncan M. Derrett
     (Berkeley and Los Angeles, 1973), p. 266. Also Robert
     Lingat, "Evolution of the Conception of Law in Burma
     and Siam," <u>Siam Society Journal</u>, 38, pt.1 (1950),
     p. 14 and following.

5.   David K. Wyatt, <u>The Politics of Reform in Thailand</u>
     (New Haven, 1969), p.8.

6.   Phra Wǫraphakphibun, <u>Prawatsat kotmai thai</u> [History
     of Thai Law] (Bangkok, 1969), p. 14; Klaus Wenk,
     <u>The Restoration of Thailand Under Rāma I, 1782-1809</u>,

28

trans. from German by Greeley Stahl (Tucson, Arizona, 1968), pp. 35-36; Prince Dhani Nivat, "The Reconstruction of Rāma I of the Chakri Dynasty," Selected Articles from the Siam Society Journal, 4 (Bangkok, 1959). p. 244.

7.   Robert Lingat suggests that the purpose of King Rama I was actually legislative rather than restorative. Because of the limitations upon the legislative power of the Thai kings, discussed in the next few pages, Rama I had to pretend that he was returning to the purity of an old text rather than creating new law for the kingdom. Lingat, "Evolution ..." p. 30.

8.   Lingat, Classical Law ..., p. 269; "Evolution ..." pp. 24-25. For a comparison of the Thai and Hindu legal texts by the Japanese legal assistant to King Chulalongkorn, see Tokichi Masao, "The Sources of Ancient Siamese Law" 15 Yale Law Journal 28 (November, 1905).

9.   This brief summary is drawn from Lingat, Classical Law..., pp. 78-79.

10.   Lingat, Classical Law..., pp. 267, 269-270; "Evolution..." pp. 15, 23-24.

11.   As translated in Akin Rabibhadana, p. 41.

12.   Phra Woraphakphibun, p. 29.

13.   David A. Wilson, Politics in Thailand (Ithaca, 1966), pp. 88-89; Akin Rabibhadana, pp. 42-43; Prince Dhani Nivat, "The Old Siamese Conception of the Monarchy," The Siam Society Fiftieth Anniversary Commemorative Publication, 2 (Bangkok, 1954), pp. 164-165.

14.   Wales, p. 17. Walter F. Vella, The Impact of the West on Government in Thailand (Berkeley, 1955), pp. 317-318.

15.   Lingat, Classical Law..., pp. 3-4.

16. See Prince Dhani Nivat, "The Old Siamese Conception of the Monarchy," p.170.

17. Lingat, "Evolution ..." p.11.

18. Lingat, Classical Law..., p. 270. See also, "Evolution..." pp. 27-28. Lingat contrasts this embryonic legislative power of the Thai kings with the Burmese system, also strongly influenced by the Mons, where no such formal procedure developed.

19. Lingat properly emphasizes the fact that King Mongkut, father of King Chulalongkorn, had already begun to adopt a new and independent attitude toward the legislative function, believing that he was not strictly bound by the sacred law as stated by Manu. "Evolution ..." p.30. See also Prince Dhani Nivat, "The Old Siamese Conception of the Monarchy," p. 172; M.R. Seni Pramoj, "King Mongkut as a Legislator," Selected Articles from the Siam Society Journal, 4 (Bangkok,1959), pp. 203-237.

20. Lucien Hanks, "Merit and Power in the Thai Social Order," American Anthropologist, 64, no.6 (December 1962), pp. 1247-1261/

21. Hanks, p. 1256.

22. Prince Dhani Nivat, "The Old Siamese Conception of the Monarchy," p. 172.

23. See David A. Wilson, p. 90.

24. Prince Phitchit Prichakǫn, "Thammasan winitchai [A Consideration of Justice] " in Prachum phraniphon krommaluang Phitchit Prichakǫn (Bangkok,1929).

25. See Wyatt, Politics of Reform..., pp. 89-90.

26. Čhaonai lae kharatchakan krap bangkhom thun khwamhen čhat kanplianplaeng ratchakan phaendin r.s. 103 [Opinions on Instituting Governmental Change

Presented to the King in 1885] (Bangkok, 1972).

27.   Phraratchadamrat tǫp khwamhen khǫng phu čha hai
plian kan pokkhrǫng [King Chulalongkorn's Reply to
the Opinions of Those Who Would Change the
Administration] pp. 51-60 of an earlier edition of the
work cited immediately above, printed for the funeral
of Mǫm Sanit Kritdakǫn (Bangkok, 1967).

28.   Throughout this paper a legal form of citation will be
used for all references to the Prachum kotmai pračham
sok, Sathian Laiyalak et al. comps., 69 vols.
(Bangkok, 1935-53), which is the yearly collection of
Thai laws and decrees. The volume number will
precede the abbreviation "PKPS". The second number
will indicate the page at which the particular law begins,
and the third number, if any, will refer to the precise
page cited. Thus 8 PKPS 211, 212, would refer to the
eighth volume of Prachum kotmai pračham sok, the
proclamation beginning at p. 211, with reference to
p. 212 in that proclamation. All such citations will
be placed in the text itself.

29.   This rough outline is based primarily upon Professor
Wyatt's study of King Chulalongkorn, Politics of
Reform ...

30.   King Chulalongkorn, Phraratchadamrat song thalaeng
phrabǫrommarachathibai kaekhai kanpokkhrǫng phaendin
[Speech Explaining the Governmental Reforms]
(Bangkok, 1927), pp. 62-63. Kasem Sirisumpundh, a
Thai political scientist, maintains that the more likely
date for this speech was 1893 rather than 1888, in
"Emergence of the Modern National State in Burma
and Thailand," Ph.D. diss. (University of Wisconsin,
1962) p. 100.

31.   Kasem Sirisumpundh and Neon Snidvongs, "Naew
phraratchadamri thang kan müang nai phrabat somdet
phra čhunlačhǫmklao čhaoyuhua [Political Thought
of King Chulalongkorn] ," Sangkomsat Parithat, 5,
no. 3 (December 1967) pp. 32-33.

32. A similar argument is advanced by Kasem Sirisumpundh alone in his doctoral dissertation, cited above.

33. Phra Sarasas, My Country Thailand (Bangkok,1960), p. 130.

34. Wales, p. 249.

35. Wales, p. 70. The actual success of King Trailok in transforming his administrative system from a territorial to a functional organization is open to some question.. Miss Ippa Hongladarom, a graduate student at the University of Michigan , South and Southeast Asia Center, has found clear suggestions to the contrary in Prince Damrong Rachanuphap, Laksana kan pokkhrọng prathet sayam tae boran [The Administration of Siam from Ancient Times] (Bangkok,1933), p. 27 and following.

36. Wales, p. 86.

37. King Chulalongkorn, Phraratchadamrat song thalaeng..., p. 3.

38. King Chulalongkorn, Phraratchadamrat song thalaeng..., pp. 4-5.

39. King Chulalongkorn, Phraratchadamrat song thalaeng..., p. 6.

40. Wales, p. 91. See also Prince Damrong, Laksana kan pokkhrọng..., p. 44.

41. King Chulalongkorn, Phraratchadamrat song thalaeng..., pp. 7-8.

42. King Chulalongkorn, Phraratchadamrat song thalaeng..., p. 11.

43. Vella, Impact of the West..., p. 326.

44. Akin Rabibhadana, p. 28; Wales, p. 127.

45. Wales, p. 74.

46. King Chulalongkorn, Phraratchadamrat song thalaeng..., pp. 13-14.

47. See King Chulalongkorn, Phraratchadamrat song thalaeng..., pp. 29-30.

48. King Chulalongkorn, Phraratchadamrat song thalaeng..., p. 42.

49. King Chulalongkorn, Phraratchadamrat song thalaeng..., p. 57.

50. Within a few years, mahatthai was to act as a genuine Ministry of the Interior with responsibilities not only in the North and Northeast but spread throughout the entire country.

51. As mahatthai's authority spread throughout the country, kalahom relinquished its regional responsibilities and involved itself only with military affairs.

52. This list is based upon King Chulalongkorn, Phraratchadamrat song thalaeng..., pp. 58-59.

53. See especially Wyatt, Politics of Reform...; and William Siffin, The Thai Bureaucracy (Honolulu, 1966). Professor Wyatt discusses King Chulalongkorn's reliance upon his own brothers as ministers rather than the powerful Bunnag family and the "old conservatives" who had previously shared control over the administrative machinery, in "Family Politics in Nineteenth Century Thailand," Journal of Southeast Asian History, 9, pt. 2, (1968), pp. 222-223.

54. From a memorandum written by King Chulalongkorn to Prince Damrong in 1895, quoted by Siffin, pp. 51-52.

55. This is the thesis of Robert Heine-Geldern in Conceptions of State and Kingship in Southeast Asia (Ithaca, 1956). The quoted phrase appears on p. 1.

CHAPTER 2

THE LEGISLATIVE FUNCTION

A. The Early Period: Privy Council and Council
   of State

On May 8, 1874 , King Chulalongkorn proclaimed
the establishment of two advisory councils to consult with him
on important matters of state and to assist in the enactment
of laws for the kingdom. 8 PKPS 154. In characteristic
fashion the king explained that the purpose of these councils
was to bring greater well-being to the people, to eradicate
old customs which served only to oppress, and to hasten the
advancement and development of the country. The king stated
that he had travelled across the sea to visit foreign lands, to
observe the customs of the more advanced nations, and to
select those practices which might prove of value and use to
Thailand. [1] The foreign origin of the advisory bodies themselves was emphasized by the transliterated English phrases
"council of state" and "privy council" used in the proclamation.

The general purpose of the advisory councils was to
discuss important matters with the king and to aid in the creation
of new laws. The king intended, according to the proclamation,
to confer with them before establishing new statutes or policies
and to solicit their suggestions or their criticisms. The members
would be free to disagree frankly with the views of the king and
need not fear any punishment for expressing their disapproval
of his ideas. Under certain conditions, moreover, the members
themselves could initiate discussion of matters they considered
important. Indeed, it was intended that the Privy Councilors,
in particular, bring defects or evils in the administration to
the attention of the king and offer their suggestions for
correction.

In a related royal edict the king provided a

statutory foundation for the new advisory councils. The Council
of State was to be composed of ten to twenty men selected by
the king on the basis of ability, reputation, and family. 8 PKPS
170 (Paragraph 1). The senabǫdi, or ministers in the
traditional bureaucratic structure, were also allowed to attend
meetings whenever the topic under discussion was relevant to
their work or whenever the king permitted them to join for any
reason. The senabǫdi were not, however, to be counted among
the original ten to twenty members. In addition to the original
councilors and the senabǫdi, six relatives of the king were also
to be appointed to the Council of State. (Paragraph 2). Any of
the councilors or the six royal relatives could be removed by
the king, and the members themselves could request such a
dismissal by a petition and letter of explanation signed by at
least six of their number. (Paragraphs 1 and 2). Resignations
required the approval of the king, and any member who resigned
from the Council was required to resign from all other
governmental positions as well. (Paragraph 24). The rank
and salary of the councilors placed them at a level below that
of the major ministers. (Paragraph 3).

Each member of the Council of State was required
to swear an oath of office before he was allowed to participate
in any of the meetings. (Paragraph 4). This oath, consisting
of seven provisions, pledged honesty, integrity, and loyalty
to the interests of the king and people. Each councilor was to
work to the best of his ability to promote the progress of the
people and to avoid disgrace to the Council. Corruption and
personal gain were to be eschewed. The secrecy of the Council's
proceedings was not to be violated. Decisions of the Council
were to be supported and strengthened, and any obstruction of
the Council's work by a fellow councilor was to be opposed.

The king himself was to act as President of the
Council, free to attend meetings or not, as he pleased.
(Paragraph 5). The other officers were the Vice-President
and the Clerk. The Vice-President, elected each year by the
membership with the king's approval, was to preside over
meetings in the king's absence. (Paragraph 6). In addition,
he was to sign important documents, count votes, act as the
Council's spokesman to the king, and resolve deadlocked
disputes when the king himself was absent. (Paragraph 7).

When the king chose not to attend meetings of the Council, he could communicate his wishes to the members by letters which were to be read by the Vice-President to the other councilors. (Paragraph 9).

The procedural rules of the Council of State were marked by two significant features: an emphasis upon free and equal discussion among the members and a requirement that voting upon legislation be unanimous. The topics for discussion were generally decided by the king and conveyed to the Council either in person or by letter. It was possible, however, for the members themselves to initiate discussion on matters which two or more wished to place before the Council. In such cases, it was necessary first to raise the issue with the king in private. If the king thought the matter appropriate for discussion he would then submit it to the Council as a whole. Proclamation, 8 PKPS 154, 156.

Unanimous approval was necessary before any measure could become law. Whenever a vote revealed that the membership was divided, each side was to restate its own point of view and the king was to approve one or the other. The proponents of the favored point of view were then to rewrite their proposal, attempting to incorporate other viewpoints as well. A second vote would then be taken, and any remaining dissenters were to offer specific suggestions for improvement. Proclamation, 8 PKPS 154, 157. It was probably believed that no strenuous objection would persist long in the face of opposition by a majority of the Council and the king himself. Moreover, behavior by any member which was regarded as particularly obstructive or improper was subject to censure by the Vice-President, the Council as a whole, or even by the king. 8 PKPS 170 (Paragraph 21).

Another procedural rule worthy of note was the participation of Privy Councilors in the meetings of the Council of State. The king could invite Privy Councilors, either individually or as a group, to attend meetings which dealt with issues related to their own work. In such cases, the Privy Councilors were permitted to participate in the discussion and the framing of laws, and to cast their votes like the Councilors of State. When the king had not requested their presence, Privy

Councilors were nevertheless allowed to attend meetings upon
written invitation by the Councilors of State if such invitations
were signed by at least six members. In the latter instance,
however, the Privy Councilors were permitted only to speak
but not to amend or revise legislation nor to participate in the
voting. (Paragraph 23).

The royal edict establishing the Privy Council,
8 PKPŞ 185, was less complex and stringent than that of the
Council of State, for the purpose of the Privy Council was advisory rather than legislative. The membership of the Privy
Council was to be composed of an indefinite number of men selected by the king from the royalty or the government bureaucracy. (Paragraph 1). These men would serve permanently in
their advisory positions, receiving no elevation in rank but an
increase in sakdina (or "dignity marks")[2] and a pension after ten
years of service. (Paragraphs 1, 2, 8). All members were required to swear an oath like that of the Councilors of State. There
was no provision for the voluntary resignation of Privy Councilors, but the king could remove members for behavior inappropriate to their station. (Paragraph 9). It was not required that
such members must then resign from all other government positions as well, as was the case for the Councilors of State.

The rules and regulations of the Council of State were
to be observed by the Privy Councilors, even in their own meetings. (Paragraph 10). In addition, the members were required
to elect a chairman for any meeting of the Council or of its committees or appointed groups. The chairman would then preside
in accordance with the procedural rules of the Council of State.
(Paragraph 11). Although it was normally forbidden to meet
without formal invitation, this was permitted in emergency situations. (Paragraph 7). It was also possible for the king to
appoint special royal commissions, whose members were selected by the king from among the Privy Councilors. Such commissions would investigate specially designated subjects and
present their findings in written form to the king. The king might
then order their reports to be read to the Privy Council as a
whole. (Paragraph 6).

In general, it was required that the Privy Councilors keep the king informed on all important matters within their
knowledge. Failure to do so was regarded as dereliction of duty.

Information presented to the king in writing must be signed by
the councilor submitting it. (Paragraph 13). In this way the
Privy Council would help the king to decide important issues
and to lead the Council of State in its work. It was imagined
that service upon the Privy Council might train young men of
ability and intelligence to aid the Council of State in later years.
Proclamation, 8 PKPS 154, 158.

Finally, a special provision was made for the establishment at the king's discretion of a Committee of the Privy
Council. This Committee would consist of members of the
Privy Council appointed by the king to function as a special
court. The Committee would be empowered to investigate
government work and to decide with judicial finality issues
involving government officials. (Paragraph 15). Decisions of
the Committee would be reached by majority vote, and both
the majority and the minority views were to be presented to
the king in writing. (Paragraph 16). Proceedings of the Committee could be conducted in public or in private, but in either
case the Committee could not prohibit the senabodi or the
Councilors of State from attending. (Paragraph 18).

Both the Privy Council and the Council of State
caused great political friction between the young and liberal
faction associated with the king and the older and more conservative forces associated with the former regent. The
conservatives resented the new system as an alien intrusion
upon the status quo aimed, they believed, at the destruction of
their own political power. Most of them refused to serve on
either council, suspecting that their influence would be out-
balanced by that of the king's own faction and fearing that their
oath of office might be used against them.[3]

In a move of some political importance, the oath of
office was indeed used as the statutory basis for dismissing
from the Privy Council the Minister of Lands in October, 1874.
8 PKPS 222. In a proclamation explaining the dismissal of
Phraya Ahanborirak from the Privy Council, King Chulalongkorn
cited three provisions of the councilor's oath which had been
violated: the pledge to advise truthfully and to the best of his
ability and intelligence in the manner most likely to promote
goodness, welfare, progress, and the high standing of the
Council itself; the pledge to act in accordance with his office

to ensure a progressive and useful reign and to promote the
welfare and morals of the people without hidden favoritism to
friends, family or relatives; and the pledge to behave in a manner appropriate to the station of Privy Councilor, that is with
goodness, honesty, love of king, and the avoidance of misdeeds.
8 PKPS 191 (Paragraphs 1, 2, 7). Contrary to this oath, the
proclamation stated, Phraya Ahanbǫrirak had not properly
performed his duties as head of the Ministry of Lands. There
was evidence that he had received funds illegally obtained by
other corrupt officials and had himself been guilty of the misappropriation of royal monies allocated to his ministry. The
king therefore exercised his power under Paragraph 9 of the
Edict of the Privy Council, 8 PKPS 185, to dismiss any member
who misused his office or performed deeds inappropriate to
his station.

To a certain extent, therefore, the statutory provisions of the two councils were applied in a literal manner,
with the king justifying his actions by the terms of these laws
rather than by reference to his powers as absolute monarch.
This practice, however, this period of experimentation, was
not to last long. The friction between the two political factions
increased with time, largely because of the refusal of the
conservative wing to participate on the councils. The increased
hostility between liberals and conseratives led directly to the
Front Palace Incident of 1874-75, and this crisis permanently
neutralized the political power of the two councils. The Front
Palace Incident marked the end of the effective functioning of
any legislative or quasi-legislative body in Thailand for the
next twenty years. [4]

Before the crisis of December 1874 and the subsequent inactivity of the Council of State and the Privy Council,
King Chulalongkorn had offered his own explanation and defense
of the new system. In three related documents the king described his conception of the legislative function at this early
stage in his reign. Whether these statements were intended
to persuade the opposition or to justify his position to the people
at large, they raised some important questions about new and
old theories of kingship.

The Council of State was justified primarily by its
record of improvements in the collecting of royal revenues.

Through improved efficiency in the accounting and collection procedures and through the replacement of corrupt revenue agents with honest new men, it was becoming possible to stop an enormous drain on government funds and to end the unworthy behavior of government officials. In this way, without adding to the tax burden upon the people, vital improvements could be financed which would benefit the people, stimulate foreign trade, and bring technological advancement to the kingdom. 8 PKPS 271.

The activities of the Privy Council were explained in more general terms by the four functions the Council was intended to perform. First, the Privy Council was to inform the king of issues which caused distress among the people so that he could raise these problems with the Council of State and the ministers and thereby alleviate them. Second, the Privy Council served as an investigating body and a forum of justice for governmental matters where a fair inquiry and disposition was required. Third, the Council served as a preparatory step for outstanding young men for whom no high governmental office was yet available but whose ability the king wished to utilize. Finally, the Council served as an example of honest government, for each member was bound by his oath to absolute integrity of action. 8 PKPS 275.

In a third and related document the king set forth two general benefits to be derived from a royal council. One such benefit was its opposition to corruption and unproductive practices. The other benefit was the council's capacity to obstruct or delay the king himself when he sought to act in a manner which was unjust or which might cause hardship to the people. 8 PKPS 269. It is questionable, however, just how seriously the king believed that his own power as monarch could be obstructed by a council which he himself created. Commentators have pointed to such phrases, together with the king's willingness to specify his powers under law, as evidence that he did indeed intend to limit his powers as absolute monarch and subordinate them to the statutory powers of bodies such as the Council of State and the Privy Council. Such conclusions, however, are probably unjustified. It was not unusual, even in the old days of the traditional kingship, for the law to require that the men serving the king "obstruct" or delay him when he sought impulsively to perform an unjust act.[5] Such opposition to the royal will did not in any sense derogate from the king's supreme role as protector and interpreter of the sacred law.

More importantly, however, the entire statutory framework of the Privy Council and the Council of State reveals an almost unlimited power of the king to control the legislative process. An analysis of the statutes themselves discloses some of the ways in which the king could dominate the workings of the two councils:

Council of State

1. The king had exclusive power to select new members. 8 PKPS 170 (Paragraph 1).
2. In addition to the ten to twenty ordinary members of the Council, the king could appoint six of his own relatives who, it may be presumed, would share his views on many issues. (Paragraph 2).
3. The king could dismiss any member, or refuse to do so, upon petition by six councilors. (Paragraph 1). It is not stated whether or not the king could dismiss members without such a petition as he did in the case of Phraya Ahanbǫrirak in the Privy Council.
4. No matter could be discussed without the prior approval of the king. If at least two members sought to raise a topic for discussion they had first to approach the king in private and seek his permission. Proclamation, 8 PKPS 154, 156.
5. If the king was absent, he could still control the meetings by official communications sent to the Vice-President to be read to the Council. (Paragraph 9).
6. The king presided over the Council as its President whenever he chose to attend its meetings. (Paragraph 5).
7. The selection of a Vice-President by vote of the members was subject to the approval of the king. (Paragraph 6).
8. The king could remove the Vice-President from office in mid-term if dissatisfied with his work. (Paragraph 6).
9. In voting by the councilors to amend or correct legislation, the king could cast the tie-breaking vote. If a voting deadlock arose in the king's absence, the matter had to be tabled. (Paragraph 19).

10. In voting by the councilors to enact legislation, agreement had to be unanimous and the king could indicate his approval or disapproval in any matter where the councilors were divided. Presumably the king also retained ultimate discretion to refuse to sign a measure even in the unlikely circumstance that the entire membership of the Council should vote against him. Proclamation, 8 PKPS 154, 157.

11. The king could add new voting members to the Council of State by inviting his Privy Councilors to attend meetings and participate in debate and in voting. Privy Councilors invited to attend by members of the Council of State, however, did not have the right to vote. (Paragraph 23).

12. The king could invite the powerful and influential senabọdi to join in meetings of the Council. (Paragraph 2).

13. No resignation became effective without the king's approval, and any resignee was required to leave his other official positions at the same time. (Paragraph 24).

14. Members who were forced to resign received lower pensions than those who resigned by choice. (Paragraph 25).

15. The oath of office was required of each member. This oath imposed obligations of honesty and integrity and also created norms of behavior which might discourage dissent among the councilors, such as the pledge to work in the interests of the king, to support the decisions of the Council, and to oppose obstructive or negative behavior by fellow members. (Paragraph 4).

Privy Council

1. The king had exclusive power to select new members, and could choose as many members as he wished. 8 PKPS 185 (Paragraph 1).

2. The king had the power to dismiss members for misuse of their position or for behavior inappropriate to their station. (Paragraph 9).

3. The members were obligated by law to inform the king of important matters within their knowledge and could be regarded as remiss in their duties for failure to do so. (Paragraph 13).

4. The Privy Council was forbidden to meet without invitation unless an emergency arose, for reasons probably related to the safety of the king. (Paragraph 7).

5. The king had exclusive power to create and staff

Royal Commissions which would investigate and report to him
on specific subjects. (Paragraph 6).

6. The king had exclusive power to establish a
Committee of the Privy Council with investigatory and quasi-
judicial powers over issues arising in the bureaucracy. The
king could appoint the Committee's Chairman if he chose, and
the Committee was required to report its findings and its
decisions to the king. (Paragraphs 15, 16, 17).

7. Each member of the Privy Council was bound
by an oath of office like that of the Councilors of State. (Paragraph 3).

8. The power of the king to control voting and
procedural matters in the Council of State would apply to the
Privy Council as well, for the same rules were used there.
(Paragraph 10).

It may be concluded that the power of the royal
councils to "obstruct" or oppose the royal will was not a re-
alistic probability with regard to the legislative function at
that time. In addition to the king's statutory controls over the
workings of the councils, there were several other factors
which prevented the councils from acting in an independent
parliamentary fashion. One was the fact that the ministers
were still a major political power and held a rank superior
to that of the councilors. Their strong opposition to any measure would surely increase the likelihood of its failure. Another
factor was the historic deference and awe accorded to the king
himself. Regardless of King Chulalongkorn's own intent to
limit his powers or to subordinate the royal prerogative to a
quasi-parliamentary system, it would be an unusual councilor
indeed who would dare to oppose any firm expression of the
royal will. Even the explicit provisions protecting the right
of the councilors to speak openly and without fear might prove
insufficiently reassuring to those whose own careers and
future well-being were dependent upon the favor of the king.[6]

B.　　The Later Period: The Legislative Council,
Provincial Legislative Powers, and the
Legislative Function During the Regency

1.　The Legislative Council

After the Front Palace Incident of 1874-1875, King
Chulalongkorn did not choose to delegate his legislative powers
again until the creation of the Legislative Council, or
ratthamontri sapha, of 1895.[7] The Legislative Council was
different from the earlier Privy Council and Council of State
not only in its longevity but in its fundamental tone and purpose.
In the establishment of the later body there was less emphasis
upon the symbolism of modernity and progress, less attention
paid to the adopting of western practices as a means to achieve
progress, no borrowing of English words and phrases to under-
line the foreign origins of the institution. The Legislative
Council was not merely an experiment but a deliberate response
to the king's need for assistance in a major restructuring of
Thailand's legal framework. The policy of gradualism and the
practice of borrowing western forms were still very much
alive; but there was now, perhaps, less faith in the potency
of the forms to effect change by themselves and more aware-
ness of the functional role these borrowed institutions were to
play in transforming Thai society.

The Legislative Council, it was announced in a
royal edict of January 10, 1895, was to supersede the old
advisory councils of 1874. 14 PKPS 213. Laws passed under
the former bodies, however, were to remain in effect.
(Clause 12). The membership of the new Council would consist
of two separate groups: all of the ministers in the newly
reorganized government bureaucracy, and twelve other men to
be selected by the king. (Clause 1). The Council was to
remain in existence at the discretion of the king. (Clause 1).
All members were required to swear a simple oath of office
pledging to perform their duties with honesty and integrity.
(Clause 4).

The chief officers of the Legislative Council were
the Chairman, Vice-Chairman, and Secretary, appointed on

a permanent basis by the king. (Clause 2). The Chairman or
Vice-Chairman would preside over all meetings (Clause 8,
Paragraph 1), but if both the Chairman and Vice-Chairman
were absent, then the senior minister would preside in their
place. (Clause 8, Paragraph 2). If no minister were present,
then the senior Council member would preside. (Clause 8,
Paragraph 2). All meetings were to be held in the Palace and
were to be convened at least once a week. (Clause 8, Paragraphs 5, 6). Voting would be determined by a simple majority,
with the presiding officer empowered to cast the tie-breaking
vote. (Clause 8, Paragraph 8). No vote would be considered
valid unless one-half of the Council members were present.
(Clause 8, Paragraph 9).

This last rule was modified twice in the next five
years, however, apparently because the business of the Council
was delayed by the absences of members who were overburdened with other duties, and by members too old or sick to
participate regularly. A royal edict of January 5, 1896
declared that in the determination of a quorum of one-half the
membership, two groups should not be counted: (a) members
absent from the capital on business in the provinces;
(b) members who, for reasons of age or health, were unable
to attend meetings regularly and were therefore to be
designated "Special rathamontri." It was emphasized that
both of these groups would retain their full rights as
ratthamontri in any meeting which they were able to attend.
15 PKPS 70. A royal edict of June 8, 1899 changed the
quorum requirement from one-half to one-fourth, while
preserving the two exceptions established by the 1896
amendment. 17 PKPS 48.

The topics which could be discussed by the Legislative Council were limited to some extent by the wishes of the
king. It was generally forbidden to discuss any matter which
the king thought inappropriate, and his wishes were made known
to the Council either by direct order or by a communication
transmitted through one of the ministers. It was also possible
for a member to raise a topic for discussion on his own
initiative, if his motion were seconded by three other members.
(Clause 6). In general, it was necessary to adhere to the
prepared agenda unless the Council voted by three-fourths of

the members in attendance to change the order of discussion or
to add a new item. (Clause 8, Paragraph 7).

The Legislative Council had the power to discuss,
debate, and reach agreement upon new laws and commands
which would promote peace, order, and good government. The
king reserved the right to impose further restrictions or
exceptions upon the Council's lawmaking power in the future.
(Clause 5). In addition, before any act could become law the
approval of the king was necessary in each instance, with a
limited exception for emergency situations. (Clause 7).
Finally, the Legislative Council was empowered to establish
special committees to consider and report to the Council on
important problems. (Clause 9).

In a speech delivered at the opening of the new
Legislative Council on January 24, 1895, King Chulalongkorn
explained his purposes in establishing the new legislative body.
14 PKPS 336. Primarily the king intended that the Council
assist him in a complete revision of the civil and criminal law,
and all other laws as well. The Council was to help him decide
the propriety of all such measures and to weigh their efficacy
in promoting the welfare, happiness, and satisfaction of the
people. The king wanted not only to protect the individual and
his property, but to increase the level of fairness, judicial
certainty and equality, and the speed and justice with which the
courts disposed of cases.

Again the king cautioned his subordinates to follow
a policy of gradualism in their approach to reform, rather than
adopting unselectively the customs of other lands. Although
change was both necessary and inevitable, the king emphasized
that certain ancient traditions must not be destroyed, for they
lay at the very core of the Thai spirit and the beliefs of the Thai
people. Although the king offered no examples of the kinds of
traditions he wished to preserve, his observations are
reminiscent of his argument in the Speech Explaining the
Governmental Reforms that the kingship itself should not be
replaced by a parliamentary system. The relationship between
the people and the king, he had asserted in the earlier speech,
was too fundamental to the Thai tradition to be tampered with,
and the people could not tolerate its alteration or destruction.

In his speech to the Legislative Council, the king alluded to the failure of the old Council of State and remarked upon his need for legislative assistance in the work that lay ahead. The king's executive responsibilities had been successfully delegated to his ministers, his commissioners and provincial governors. His judicial responsibilities had been carried out with the assistance of the various officers of the judiciary. His legislative responsibilities, however, had not been delegated to anyone since the days of the Council of State, and as a result they had gone largely unperformed. It was the king's intention, therefore, to establish the Legislative Council as a permanent body which would, as the king's designated agent, perform the legislative function of the Thai monarch. Even if the king were travelling outside the kingdom, or were ill and unable to work, the Legislative Council would be able to function without any interruption.

It is this last point which raises an important question as to the powers of the Legislative Council. This question concerns the capacity of the Council not only to discuss, draft, and approve legislation, but to enact it as law. In his speech, King Chulalongkorn employed an ambiguous phrase to describe the power of the Council to promulgate laws in the king's absence, a phrase which may be translated roughly as, "Bills which have been consulted and agreed upon may be enacted as laws." The ambiguity lies in the uncertainty as to whether the consultation and agreement must involve the king, or whether the Council itself could enact the bill without his prior approval. This point was clarified in Clause 7 of the royal edict establishing the Legislative Council. According to its provisions, no bill could normally become law without the king's approval. If the king were absent or incapacitated, however, and there was need for swift enactment, a law would become effective when it was proclaimed even without the prior approval of the king. To this emergency power of the Council, however, three important conditions were appended: (a) at least half of the total membership of the Legislative Council and three-quarters of the members present at the meeting must have clearly agreed upon the law and the need for emergency action; (b) the law could not conflict with the royal power and dignity; it could not infringe upon the sovereignty or integrity of the country; it could not violate or conflict with any foreign treaty; it could not give away land, money, or other property; it could not abolish or establish any tax; (c) the king had the power to repeal such laws at any time he wished.

It was clearly the intent of the king that the work of the Legislative Council remain subject to his scrutiny and his veto. Even when the king was absent, the ability of the Council to promulgate laws without prior approval by the king was sharply limited and subject to immediate review upon the king's return to work. This body was not yet the parliament envisioned by the eleven petitioners who asked in 1887 that the king establish a constitutional monarchy. It was not a machine which could function smoothly even in the absence of the king, nor did it remove the king from his position of overwhelming importance in the legislative function. The fact that the king was still able to exercise almost total control over the legislative process is evidenced by a list of the statutory powers which the king retained in relation to the Legislative Council:

Legislative Council

1. The king had exclusive power to select members of the Legislative Council. 14 PKPS 213 (Clause 1).
2. The king could dissolve the Legislative Council at any time, for it lasted only as long as he required its assistance. (Clause 1).
3. All members were obliged to swear an oath of office, pledging to perform their statutory duties with honesty and integrity. (Clause 4).
4. The power of the Council to debate and agree upon bills was subject to any restriction of scope which the king might choose to impose upon the body's lawmaking capacity. (Clause 5).
5. The king could forbid the discussion of matters he deemed inappropriate for Council consideration. A council member could propose new topics for discussion if his initiative was supported by three other members, but it must be presumed that such an initiative would be forced to yield to an explicit prohibition by the king. (Clause 6).
6. In their discussions, the members could not

depart from their predetermined agenda without an affirmative vote of three-fourths of the members in attendance. (Clause 8, Paragraph 7).

7. Under normal conditions, no bill became effective as law until (a) a writing by the king signified his approval, (b) the royal seal was affixed, and (c) the law was officially proclaimed. (Clause 7).

8. In an emergency such as the king's absence or incapacity, the Legislative Council could enact measures into law without his prior approval, but this power was subject to the severe restrictions enumerated above, and to the possibility of a later veto by the king upon his return. (Clause 7).

9. The minutes of all meetings were to be sent to the king within fifteen days. (Clause 8, Paragraph 10).

10. The king had exclusive power to appoint the Chairman, the Vice-Chairman, and the Secretary of the Legislative Council. (Clause 2).

11. The presiding officer of the Legislative Council, usually either the Chairman or Vice-Chairman selected by the king, had the power to cast a tie-breaking vote if necessary. (Clause 8, Paragraph 8).

12. Meetings of the Legislative Council were held in the royal palace, close to the king's scrutiny and influence. (Clause 8, Paragraph 5).

Because the king exercised such strict control over the legislative process, it is instructive to search for areas where the king's supervision might be less intense, where more freedom might be given to institutions or people outside his immediate influence to play a creative part in the development of new law. Two such areas worthy of examination are the legislative powers of the provincial authorities and of the government under the queen as regent during the king's European travels. In both instances, necessity demanded that the legislative function be delegated beyond the king's direct control. Both examples represent the outer limits of the king's willingness to see laws enacted without his prior approval.

2. Provincial Legislative Powers and
    the Legislative Function During
    the Regency

Under normal circumstances, the function of
local government was not to enact new laws but to enforce
statutes promulgated by the king. In the Law of Provincial
Administration enacted by King Chulalongkorn on May 20, 1897,
no independent legislative power was given to any official at
the village, tambon, or district level.[8] 16 PKPS 22. The
role of the local officials at these lower levels was purely
executive and not legislative.

In the case of the monthon, however, the largest
administrative unit outside the capital, and its sub-unit the
müang, or province, a limited legislative power was granted
to the administrative officers. In an order issued by the
Ministry of Justice on August 29, 1900, the ordinary and the
emergency legislative powers of the Chief Commissioner
(khaa luang yai) and the Commissioner of Justice (khaa luang
yutitham) for the Northwest monthon were elaborated. The
monthon administrators were permitted, under normal
circumstances, to draft legislation when both the Chief
Commissioner and the Commissioner of Justice concurred as
to its necessity and propriety. Such legislation was then to be
sent to Bangkok, and with the king's approval it became law.
In emergencies, when both the Chief Commissioner and the
Commissioner of Justice agreed that exceptional circumstances
required immediate action, then they could enact laws without
the king's prior approval. This emergency power was,
however, limited by the following restrictions: (a) the law
was still to be sent to the king for post facto approval within
six months from the date of enactment; (b) such laws could not
impose a penalty in excess of 200 baht or six months imprisonment; (c) such laws could not conflict with the royal power or
with any foreign treaty.

Officials at the müang level in the Northwest monthon
were also given a limited power to legislate. When such officials
agreed together upon the necessity for some law, presumably a
criminal prohibition of some type, they were empowered to

enact it if the penalty did not exceed 100 baht or three months
imprisonment. Such laws, however, could not conflict with
any law of the central government nor with any treaty. A law
enacted by müang officials would not become effective until
approved by both the Chief Commissioner and the Commissioner
of Justice in the Northwest monthon, and all such laws were to
be sent to Bangkok for the king's approval within six months.
17 PKPS 452.

A similar power to enact laws under ordinary and
emergency conditions was granted to the monthon of Phuket
in a proclamation signed by the Minister of the Interior on
February 8, 1905. 19 PKPS 359. It may therefore be
assumed that such a delegation of legislative powers was not
unusual during King Chulalongkorn's reign. Indeed, in neither
of the instances described here did the king consider the delegation of such legislative power worthy even of his personal
signature, for both enactments were issued at the ministerial
level. It should be stressed, too, that the Chief Commissioner,
the Commissioner of Justice, and the müang governor were all
appointed by the central administration in Bangkok and were
considered agents of the central government working in the
provinces, rather than representatives of the local population.

In the far South a slightly different situation
prevailed. The semi-autonomous Muslim areas at the turn
of the century were only gradually being assimilated into the
central legal framework. For this reason, an order issued
by Prince Damrong of the Ministry of the Interior on December
10, 1901 gave a special legislative authority to the old Muslim
princes, now transformed into müang governors. 18 PKPS 197.
Under this order, the administrative unit in each müang,
composed of the governor, the assistant governor, the yokkrabat,
and an assistant administrator, was specifically permitted to
enact laws and administrative orders which they considered
necessary and appropriate. Such laws could not, however,
infringe upon the royal power, nor conflict with any existing
law of the central Thai government or with any treaty. It was
required, moreover, that all laws so enacted meet with the
approval of a Commissioner specially appointed for the seven
Muslim provinces. (Paragraphs 2 and 4). Under emergency
conditions, when immediate action was necessary, any member

of the müang administrative unit was empowered to issue a
provisional order. He was then required to inform the other
members, who could approve or disapprove the order in their
next meeting. (Paragraph 9).

To summarize, then, a limited legislative power
was permitted to exist at the müang and monthon levels. It
was exercised, however, by officials of the central government
rather than representatives of the local populace, with the
notable exception of the Muslim officials in the far South.
Prior approval by the king was the rule, with a narrow exception granted in emergencies, when laws of limited scope could
be enacted immediately but were then to be sent to Bangkok
for approval. At the müang level, minor laws could be
enacted with the approval of the monthon government and, later,
of the king. Again, the Muslim provinces were a significant
exception, and there the local legislative power appeared to be
more extensive.

Generally speaking, therefore, the legislative
power existing outside of Bangkok was permitted as an
administrative necessity. It was an acknowledgement by the
central government of the realities of distance and time and,
in the case of the Muslim provinces, of a strongly autonomous
body of local tradition. The delegation of legislative power to
the provinces was intended to maximize the effectiveness of
the central government's administration in those areas, and
was not intended to provide an opportunity for each locality to
exercise its own indigenous powers of legislative creativity.
The control of the king over all laws drafted in the provinces
was maintained to the utmost extent possible. Only to a very
slight degree, if at all, could the local legislative powers be
said to detract from the king's strong control over the
legislative function.

A second area of delegated legislative responsibility
was the government of the queen as regent during the king's
two European tours. The significant departure from normal
legislative procedure here lay in the fact that, in certain
instances, measures drafted by the Legislative Council could
be enacted into law without the king's prior approval. The king
himself expressed a strong desire that the business of government

should be carried on as usual in his absence. He emphasized, in a proclamation of March 14, 1897, that new legislation which became necessary while he was in Europe should not be delayed until his return, but should be proposed and enacted immediately as it would be were the king still present. Although he suggested that any official with a reform presently in mind should inform the king before his departure, he also insisted that matters which arose after he left should not be allowed to accumulate, for then an unmanageable backlog of work would confront him upon his return. 15 PKPS 261.

In a royal ordinance of March 21, 1897, King Chulalongkorn provided for the functioning of the government in his absence. 15 PKPS 251. Queen Saowapha was to serve as regent, and five officials were appointed as her special advisers. (Clauses 2, 3). Decisions of these advisers were to be reached by a majority vote, with the Queen or the presiding officer empowered to cast a tie-breaking vote. (Clause 10). The legislative function was to be performed by the Legislative Council as it had been in the past. The only change was in the method by which laws were approved and promulgated. This process was to be a joint responsibility of the queen, her advisers, and the ministers, all of whom were required to sign any law passed by the Council before it could become effective. (Clause 17). There was a requirement that, if any emergency arose which the queen was unable to handle, an attempt should be made to contact the king in Europe. (Clause 4). This provision could be interpreted as a restriction upon major new legislative activity. In general, however, the approval of the queen was to be considered binding like that of the king, so long as no law infringed upon the royal power or traditions, the sovereignty, security and unity of the country, nor conflicted with any foreign treaty, and so long as such laws were in each instance discussed with the advisers and signed by the proper parties. (Clause 6). The fact that significant legislation was indeed enacted during this period is evidenced by laws such as a proclamation of June 21, 1897, enacted under the regency and signed by the queen, which substantially modified the structure and operation of the provincial courts. 16 PKPS 71.

In the case of the regency government, as in that of the provincial governments, the king yielded to the demands of necessity and provided that the legislative function be performed without his total supervision and control. In the case of the regency, in particular, it should be noted that the group which held the power to enact legislation into law was as close to the king as possible: his own queen, a group of advisers specially chosen by the king for this purpose, and ministers appointed by the king himself. The time during which the king delegated this responsibility was, moreover, sharply limited, and provision was made for communication with the king in the event that any emergency should arise. In short, the government of the regency did not, any more than the government in the provinces, represent a substantial departure from the normal legislative pattern established by King Chulalongkorn in the later years of his reign.

3. Comparisons with the Parliamentary System

One commentator has observed that the Legislative Council, after functioning actively for some ten years, appeared to end its effective work in 1907, after which no meetings are recorded. He speculates that the king chose to end the Council's existence rather than see it remain as a permanent body with a power potentially threatening to the legislative prerogative of the king himself:

> It is quite possible that when the great press of new legislation was over in 1907, the king allowed the council to wither rather than risk the development of a permanent institution to challenge the royal will. [9]

This interpretation conflicts with a view commonly advanced that the Legislative Council was intended by the king as a "pre-Parliament," as a training for the Thai nation in parliamentary procedure which would later come to fruition in the form of a constitutional system. Indeed, the same commentator observes elsewhere that whatever the king's intention, the Legislative Council served to "humanize the throne" and, by transforming the king into a mere "president of the administration," began a process which was to end in revolution against the absolute rule of King Chulalongkorn's "less-commanding" successors. [10]

It is interesting to speculate upon the questions of royal motive and intent, and upon the changing image of the king as legislator in the eyes of his subordinates and subjects. Such speculation should not, however, lead to erroneous depictions of the Legislative Council or of the earlier advisory bodies as "pre-Parliaments" in the legal sense of the word. In each case the king retained an insurmountable control over the personnel, the procedures and functions, and the very existence of the bodies in question. There is little justification for asserting that the establishment of a constitutional government in Thailand in 1932 represented a continuity from the beginnings of parliamentarism under King Chulalongkorn. It was, on the contrary, a sharp break from the traditional system of king as legislator.

A few examples from the provisional constitution of June 1932 will demonstrate the extent to which the revolution reversed the traditional powers of king and legislators:

Provisional Constitution of 1932

1. Although the king remained the highest leader of the country in whose name all government work was carried out, he was only one of four organs of government representative of the supreme power of the people. The other three governmental organs were the Parliament, the State Council (a fifteen-man body selected by a Chairman who was himself elected by the members of Parliament), and the Courts. 45 PKPS 131 (Clauses 1, 2, 3, 32, and 33).
2. No action of the king was valid under law unless there also appeared the signature of some member of the State Council with the approval of the Council as a whole. (Clause 7).
3. Parliament had the power to write royal acts which became law with the signature of the king. If the king should object to any law and refuse to sign it, the Parliament could approve the law a second time at which point it would

take effect despite the king's objection. (Clause 8).

4. It was the responsibility of Parliament, rather than the king, to oversee the affairs of the country and to dismiss any member of the State Council or the government bureaucracy. (Clause 9).

5. The ministers were responsible to the State Council rather than to the king and could not lawfully act in contravention of any order or rule of the State Council nor any provision of the Constitution. (Clause 31). Although the king held the power to appoint and dismiss the ministers, he could do so only with the advice of the State Council. (Clause 35).

6. Members of Parliament were not selected by the king. Initially they were to be selected by the military section of the ruling People's Party. Within six months, or whenever conditions in the country returned to normal, the Parliament would be composed of two groups of equal number. The first group would be elected by the people, while the second group would be appointed by the military section of the People's Party as before. When at least half of the country's population had passed the elementary education test, or else within ten years of the enactment of the Provisional Constitution, all members of Parliament would be popularly elected. (Clause 10).

7. The king had no power to remove members of Parliament, but this power could be exercised by the Parliament itself when it judged that the presence of any member was detrimental to the body as a whole. (Clause 16).

8. The making of treaties and the power of declaring wars were powers of the king, but they could be exercised only with the advice of the State Council. (Clauses 36, 37).

It is apparent from this list of examples drawn from the Provisional Constitution of June 1932, that the legislative function as established under King Chulalongkorn had been totally inverted. Near-total control by the king over the legislative body was replaced with near-total control by the Parliament over the king. The power of the people was theoretically supreme, and this power augmented the political strength of the Parliament and its State Council rather than the king.

King Chulalongkorn had greatly enlarged the

legislative function of the traditional monarchy under the rule
of the thammasat:

> The king's traditional duty of adhering to
> the Thammasat, or basic law, was sub-
> verted byChulalongkorn in his reforma-
> tion of the structure and functions of the
> Thai government. The Thai king was no
> longer just an executor of traditional law;
> he became a legislator with unlimited
> powers to change Thai government and
> Thai life. [11]

In expanding the legislative powers of the king, however,
King Chulalongkorn established no pattern of mutuality or
balanced power between executive and legislator for the
revolutionary government to follow. In this sense the
expanded legislative function under King Chulalongkorn
represented a consummation of the old order rather than a
prelude to the new.

NOTES

1. During the regency period King Chulalongkorn had twice travelled abroad. The first trip, in March of 1871, took him to Singapore, Batavia, and Semarang. The second trip, in December of the same year, included among other places Singapore, Burma, and India.

2. The sakdina system was one of four systems, according to Akin Rabibhadana, which were used to "distinguish the power and dignity of the officials." The other three systems were: "the yot (rank in form of title), the ratchathinnam (honorific name), and the tamnaeng (official position)." p. 102. The sakdina system itself is described by Ajaan Akin in the following terms:

    > The sakdina (dignity marks) system was a device which served as the most accurate guide to the different statuses of the whole population. Its main function was to serve as a guide for behavior in interactions.... (T)he amount of sakdina one possessed correlated with the amount of manpower under one's control. The control of manpower brought two assets which were wealth and political power.... Thus the ranking system as shown in the sakdina was based mainly on wealth and political power. p. 98.

3. Wyatt, Politics of Reform ..., p. 56.

4. See generally Professor Wyatt's account of this period of political friction and crisis, Politics of Reform ..., pp. 57-62.

5. In the kot monthianban section of the Law of the Three Seals, two provisions illustrate the duty of the king's

servants to obstruct or delay him when he sought to pursue a wrongful course of action:

The first provision, 2 PKPS 128, required that any person who disagreed with the king on any official matter should express his dissent at least three times in public audience. If the king was not persuaded, then the dissenter was required to follow the king and discuss the matter privately with him before acquiescing to the royal will. Failure to follow the terms of this provision was a violation of the law.

The second provision, 2 PKPS 129, stated that, if the king should become angry with any person and call for a weapon, it was forbidden for members of his court to provide him with it. Violation of this rule was punishable by death.

This analogy between the Law of the Three Seals and the role of King Chulalongkorn's advisory councils was pointed out by Ajaan Nidhi Aeusrivongse.

6. See Vella, Impact of the West..., p. 338.

7. King Chulalongkorn created a governmental Cabinet on April 1, 1892. Since its functions were primarily executive, it is not considered here as a participant in the legislative function. See Wyatt, Politics of Reform ..., pp. 94-101.

8. The five units of provincial administration were, in order of increasing size: (1) muu ban (village); (2) tambon (comparable to a precinct); (3) amphoe (district); (4) müang (province); (5) monthon (region).

9. David A. Wilson, p. 197.

10. David A. Wilson, p. 103.

11. Vella, Impact of the West..., p. 349.

CHAPTER 3

THE JUDICIAL FUNCTION

A. Transformation of the Judiciary

There were several reasons why a restructuring of the Thai judiciary lay at the heart of King Chulalongkorn's plan of reforms. A primary consideration was Thailand's foreign policy dilemma. In order to secure for herself an unassailable position among the "civilized" nations of the world, free from the threat of invasion by the aggressive western colonialists, Thailand had to transform the administration and substance of her laws into a pattern recognized and accepted by the great world powers. In this way, too, the insult to Thai sovereignty represented by the extraterritorial courts might be removed. A domestic consideration was the king's desire to improve the well-being of his people and to protect them from corrupt, wasteful and arbitrary judicial practices. By restructuring the judiciary the king could also increase his control over the country's affairs, in the provinces as well as in Bangkok. Since the waning of the patriarchal monarchy, the direct involvement of the king in individual cases seems to have been partially superseded by the Brahmin legal experts who were responsible for interpreting the ancient law.[1] By reforming the judiciary, the king would be able to assert his influence and imprint his policies upon each level of the judicial process and thereby extend the power of the central administration throughout the country.

King Chulalongkorn's foreign advisers played an important role in this regard, and the Belgian Adviser-General Rolin-Jacquemyns, in particular, left an indelible mark upon the judicial reforms of the period. It was he who urged upon the king the importance of an effective local government and judiciary in implementing the wishes of the people. He was disturbed by the failure of local leaders to seize criminals or to deal adequately with other problems which caused aggravation

59

and hardship to the common people. He emphasized to the king
the frequency with which corruption among judges obstructed
the workings of justice, for bribes were commonly offered to
prevent the trial or punishment of criminal defendants. These
shortcomings created among the people a general distrust of
the Thai government which, according to Rolin-Jacquemyns,
made the country ripe for foreign intervention.[2] For reasons
such as these, the king came to believe that a reorganization
of the Thai judiciary was essential to the security of the
country, to his own political control, and to the well-being of
the people.

1. Historical Perspective

King Chulalongkorn inherited a judicial system the
chief characteristic of which was the division of responsibility.
Nearly thirty different courts were scattered among the
various ministries and departments, with overlapping jurisdiction and uncertain lines of authority and supervision. Since
the ministry heads were not legal experts, the courts were
isolated from any effective control over their functions. The
powers of these courts evolved largely without concern as to
the rationality of the system as a whole, and the result was
chaotic. The king himself found it difficult to trace the
tangled lines of judicial development and to explain the many
anomalies of jurisdiction and procedure which history and
accident had imbedded in the Thai court system.[3] It is not
difficult to imagine the despair of the average citizen when
forced to confront a judiciary so complex and potentially
threatening to his own well-being.

Responsibility was divided not only among the various
ministries and departments but within the very process of
adjudication itself. Although the trial was conducted by a judge,
or tralakan, the merits and justiciability of each case were
decided by a permanent body of officials known as the lukkhun
(or lukkhun na san luang). This unit, a separate department
in the traditional bureaucracy, was composed of a small group
of Brahmin legal specialists.[4] The lukkhun played a crucial
but limited role in the judicial procedure. They could interpret
the mysteries of the law but could neither administer nor

execute it. They were consulted at several stages during the
litigation: upon receipt of the original suit at the department
for receiving plaints, upon the completion of a preliminary
hearing, and at the end of the presentation of evidence. Yet it
was the tralakan who presided at the trial and who delivered
the final verdict-- after the lukkhun had ruled on the merits
and after the official in charge of punishments had fixed a
suitable penalty for the losing party. [5]   This cumbersome
procedure created numerous opportunities for delay and
exposed the litigant at each phase of the adjudicatory process
to the danger of improper influence.

Ironically, this bifurcated judicial system may itself
have resulted from the reform of an older system where the
lukkhun exercised total control over the entire legal process.
As hypothesized by King Chulalongkorn himself, this earlier
and more unified approach may have been abandoned during the
reign of King Trailok of Ayutthaya, because the lukkhun had
lost their legal expertise and influence and were unable to
administer the judicial system efficiently. In creating his new
system of ministries and departments, King Trailok gave the
responsibility for supervising the courts and the trial process
to the various departments of the bureaucracy. He allowed the
lukkhun to retain the power to render verdicts only after the
trial had already been conducted elsewhere. [6]

Another important feature of the traditional judicial
system was the absence of a clear distinction between civil
and criminal cases. Cases involving issues which, in other
legal systems, would be regarded as criminal matters, were
brought before the court by the injured party as plaintiff. His
remedy might consist not only of a money judgement or a return
of stolen property, but of the punishment of the defendant by the
local authorities. Civil and criminal elements were thus
combined in a single lawsuit. It was permissible, moreover,
for the plaintiff and defendant to reach a settlement without
going to trial in all "criminal" cases except those involving
certain offenses of unusual gravity. If the parties agreed not
to litigate such major offenses, then the head of the department
in which the trial took place was required to inform the king and
await his instructions or, if the case was tried in the provinces,
to seek similar orders from the provincial governor. [7]   There

was thus some assurance that the perpetrators of serious crimes could not escape punishment merely because their victim had been persuaded not to bring suit.

The administration of justice in the provinces, under the traditional legal system, was apparently similar to that in the capital. Each department with administrative responsibilities in a given region also established courts to try cases which fell within their jurisdiction. The role of the lukkhun, however, seems for the most part to have been performed by the provincial governor and the provincial council. After the tralakan conducted the trial, the provincial governor and council would render the verdict and pronounce sentence. Appeals from provincial cases were handled at the local level in most instances before any authority in the central government could be approached. Errors of the tralakan could be raised before the provincial governor and council. Errors of the council could be reviewed by any member who did not participate in the original decision. Appeals against the governor himself went directly to the luang or royal court in Bangkok, after the local court had been informed that such an appeal was to be raised. In this process, the yokkrabat acted as a check on unfair or illegal behavior by the governor or his council and reported independently to the king on such matters. [8]

In the provinces, the political power of the governor was probably strong enough to influence the decisional process in the local courts. The only recourse for a litigant adversely affected by such influence was a lengthy and expensive appeal to the distant Bangkok courts. In the provinces and in Bangkok, the problems of delay and improper influence were multiplied with each additional stage in the process of litigation. The cumbersome and confusing judicial system, the expenses, delays and personal dangers involved in litigation, the traditional respect and fear of official authority were all factors which might have discouraged local citizens from seeking justice in the traditional courts of Thailand or from daring to correct official abuses when they occurred.

2. Structural Reorganization of the
Judiciary under King Chulalongkorn

a. The Early Period

King Chulalongkorn's first attempts to cure the confusion and ineffectiveness of the judiciary were, like his early experiments with new legislative bodies, short-lived. In 1874 he resorted to an instrument of royal control over the judicial function known as the rap sang court, a temporary court created by and accountable to the king for the resolution of a particular case or group of cases. The rap sang court was established by royal edict on July 14, 1874 to decide cases pending in the four major ministries-- mahatthai, kalahom, tha (khlang), and nakhonban. 8 PKPS 162. This court, which had been suggested by the Council of State, was intended to alleviate the problem of increased crime throughout the country, and to assist the nakhonban ministry whose chief was ill and whose work was not being completed. It is also likely, however, that the rap sang court was intended as a radical challenge to the traditional court system, with the ultimate purpose of ending the delay, expense and corruption which had become endemic in the courts of the major ministries. [9]

The edict establishing the rap sang court dealt primarily with major crimes of violence, both in Bangkok and the provinces. It required that all cases of any type then pending trial at nakhonban be transferred to the rap sang court. The court would then retain those suits involving major offenses and redirect the petty offenses to an official in nakhonban for speedy decision. The heads of mahatthai, kalahom, and tha were ordered to do the same for all cases then pending in their departments which had arisen in the provinces and been sent on to Bangkok. In this way the rap sang judges, who were directly accountable to the king, would acquire jurisdiction over most of the important cases then pending in the Bangkok courts and, at least in the case of nakhonban suits, would apparently retain such jurisdiction on a semi-permanent basis.

The fact that the king's motive went beyond mere criminal punishment is evidenced by several provisions which were aimed at the elimination of improper influence and corruption in the judicial process. In Paragraph 5, for example, it was made a punishable offense to coach the defendant during the trial, to announce during the trial that the defendant had friends in high positions, or to obstruct the process of justice in any other way. Paragraph 7 required that the king be informed of any instance in which a defendant or a witness could not be brought before the trial court because he resided in the royal palace, in the house of a senabọdi, or in the residence of a prince or high government official. In all of these situations there was a likelihood that the influence of status and power might prevent the trial from taking place. Paragraph 10 prohibited private communications between litigants and judges in the rap sang court which might serve as channels for bribery and corruption.

The rap sang court, not surprisingly, created resentment among those who had long depended on the traditional system for their livelihood. It was threatening not only because it removed many cases from courts where jurisdiction had previously been exercised, but also because it announced new standards of behavior to be observed by judges and by litigants. The edict was modified and weakened after the Front Palace Incident of 1874-1875, during the same period when King Chulalongkorn's early legislative reforms were to enter a period of quiescence. [10]

The king also attempted in three different ways to solve the problem of appeals, linked as it was to difficulties of political power and influence. His first step was to alter the procedure for appeal in provincial cases where the governor and provincial council had acted as the primary stage in the reviewing process. In 1874 the king proclaimed that, in any ministry or department which had its own court, the athibọdi who was head of that department should hear all complaints against the provincial council, the governor, the lukkhun, the tralakan, and others. If the athibọdi should fail to render a decision on the matter, then the case could go directly to the king by petition. 8 PKPS 257. The king wanted the athibọdi in each department to use his influence to ensure the speed and fairness of appeals which would otherwise pass through the complexities of the provincial appellate system and the luang court of appeals. This plan, as he later admitted, failed because the athibǫdi were reluctant to exercise their political power in this manner. Instead, they usually evaded their responsibilities by designating a new tralakan to hear the cases and send them on to the lukkhun for a verdict.[11] The king was unable to make use of the status and power of the athibǫdi in his efforts to expedite appeals from trial court errors and abuses. The appellate process simply became slower and more convoluted, with considerable confusion arising as to the respective appellate functions of the athibǫdi and the luang appeals court.

During this same period the king appointed an official known as the mae kǫng, who was to examine sentences imposed upon defendants before such sentences were reviewed by the king himself. The king apparently intended that the mae kǫng would screen all cases which were to be presented for royal review and thereby dispose of the litigation with greater speed and efficiency. Instead, however, the mae kǫng neglected to review most of these cases because he lacked the political power to do so. Litigants began to appeal to the mae kǫng as a matter of form merely to delay the final disposition of each case. If the mae kǫng ever managed to decide a case, his decision was then appealed automatically for a second examination by the king himself. Instead of expediting the review of cases at the high-est level, the mae kǫng merely delayed them further. In a proclamation of 1885, the king recognized this difficulty and abolished the office of mae kǫng as an intermediate step in the process of royal review. 10 PKPS 16; 10 PKPS 244.[12]

In a final attempt to establish a body with sufficient power and status to decide the cases brought before it, the king formed a dika court to assist him in deciding petitions for royal review. This court was composed of relatives of the king who, by reason of status and intimacy with the king himself, might have been expected to wield the influence necessary to bring order to the judicial system. Again, however, the king was forced to admit failure. At that time it appeared that no one except the king himself possessed the power to decide litigation with an authority and finality respected even by the most influential parties.[13]

In his Speech Explaining the Governmental Reforms the king described in the most negative terms the situation then existing in the Thai judiciary. Although the athibọdi were given responsibility to ensure the efficient operation of the courts under their control, they lacked the power to force defendants and witnesses of high status to submit to the court's jurisdiction. The tralakan, in consultation with the lukkhun, were instead obliged to seek the aid of the police whom the king had specifically empowered to assist the trial courts in such matters. If, however, the courts were still unable to proceed or to render verdicts because of other obstacles which arose, then they were forced to come to the king himself and request a royal command that the defendant appear before the court and comply with the normal court procedures.

In short, the king complained, he was overburdened with the day-to-day details of the judicial function to the extent that he was unable to perform his other duties as king. At the same time, he had failed in every attempt to delegate his various judicial responsibilities to some other person or institution, from the rap sang court, to the athibọdi of the various departments, to the mae kọng for screening royal petitions, to the dika court composed of his own relatives. Each attempt to bring greater efficiency and honesty to the judicial process had instead brought greater waste and delay. The Thai judiciary, said the king, was like a merchant ship which was fully loaded but rotten and decayed. Until the present time, each hole had been plugged as it became apparent, but the decay had continued and the cargo was increasingly damaged. It was time, he concluded, to build a new vessel out of stronger planks.[14]

b. The Ministry of Justice and the Bangkok Courts

On March 25, 1892 King Chulalongkorn proclaimed the establishment of a new Ministry of Justice and a streamlined organization for the Bangkok courts. 13 PKPS 74. He was, he announced, determined to end the delay and corruption which resulted from the divided judicial responsibilities of the old system. His solution was to regroup all the Bangkok courts under one minister who would oversee the judicial process, resolve important problems which arose, and make certain that the procedure was both convenient and just. The division of responsiblity between the tralakan and lukkhun was also changed. In charge of each of the new courts was an athibǫdi, or chief judge, whose role it was to decide the cases and to supervise the trial process. Under him was a staff of examiners who would actually conduct the trials. (Paragraph 4). The practice of sending the case out of the court to a separate lukkhun department for a verdict was thereby eliminated. Each case was to be supervised from beginning to end by the athibǫdi of the court in which it was brought.

Seven courts were established under the proclamation to replace the numerous courts which formerly existed in the various ministries. The new courts were: (1) Royal Appeals Court (performing the appellate function of the dika court), (2) People's Appeals Court (replacing the mahatthai appeals court), (3) Court for Punishable Offenses, (4) phaeng kasem court (a civil court), (5) phaeng klang court (a civil court), (6) sanphakǫn court (a tax and inheritance court), (7) International (extraterritorial) Courts. A department was also established within the Ministry of Justice to receive all plaints brought by the people. Its function was to channel the suits into the appropriate courts and to prevent the parties from exercising improper influence upon the athibǫdi of the court by bringing their pleadings directly to him. As time went on, however, this department caused more problems than it resolved. Many would-be litigants misunderstood its function and believed that their suits had been disallowed because of corruption within the judiciary, although in fact the department had rejected the pleadings on technical grounds. When a later effort of the king to clarify the work of the department had failed, 13 PKPS 166, he finally abolished it entirely and established new standards for receiving plaints in each court. 13 PKPS 178.

Other adjustments also proved necessary as the new system was put to actual use. In the same edict in which the king abolished the department to receive plaints, he also abolished the Royal Appeals Court with an explanation that there were not enough appeals brought by the people to justify two separate appeals courts. This left only the People's Appeals Court as a body which would review trial court decisions in Bangkok. From this court, appeals could be taken by royal petition directly to the king. 13 PKPS 178 (Paragraph 1).

It was also found that the number of cases involving punishable offenses was too great for a single court to handle. For this reason a new forum was created, the ratchathanphichet court, which would decide half of the cases then pending before the Court for Punishable Offenses, and would continue to share the case load which would arise in the future. 13 PKPS 178 (Paragraph 2). On January 4, 1896, however, the ratchathanphichet court was abolished. It was provided at the same time that a similar court might later be revived if the necessity should ever arise again. In the same proclamation the two "civil" courts, the phaeng kasem court and the phaeng klang court, were merged into one civil court. 15 PKPS 68 By 1896, then, the major courts in the Ministry of Justice were: (1) People's Appeals Court, (2) Court for Punishable Offenses, (3) "Civil" Court, (4) sanphakon court, (5) the International Courts.

It is interesting to note as well the development from 1893 to 1896 of a "misdemeanors" court for the city of Bangkok. The porisapha (also called polisapha) court was established by royal edict on March 31, 1893. 13 PKPS 237. It was not until nearly two years later, however, that this court came to be used as an experimental model for several new judicial rules and practices which were later to be employed in the major courts of the entire country. In a proclamation of December 25, 1894 the king announced the establishment of three more porisapha courts in the city of Bangkok. 14 PKPS 206. Each of the four courts was to decide petty cases arising in its own quadrant of the city, the precise geographical boundaries of which were announced on February 26, 1895. 14 PKPS 292.

In the proclamation of December 25, 1894, there appeared for the first time a precise statement of the way in which a court acquired jurisdiction over a suit brought before it. The court in each quadrant could assert jurisdiction over

a case: (a) if the cause of action arose in that quadrant; (b) if
the defendant's domicile was located in that quadrant; or (c) if
that court had already decided another closely related case.
The proclamation also described the manner in which the judge
should announce his verdict to the parties. In particular it
required that the judge explain the reasons for his decision and
the law on which he had relied, together with specific findings
of fact. Other details of judicial procedure were also described with a degree of precision not to be found in most laws of
that time. On August 11, 1895, one of the four porisapha
courts was abolished because there were not enough cases to
justify its continued existence. 15 PKPS 12. The role of the
porisapha courts as experimental models, however, was to
continue. On January 13, 1896 a new rule was proclaimed for
all courts in the Ministry of Justice. Trial court sentences
inflicting up to fifty lashes as punishment for violations of the
law were prohibited and were to be replaced by the imprisonment of the guilty party. This modification of the law, it was
announced, had first been tested in the porisapha courts where
it had proved a useful solution, at least in part, to the
troubling problem of corporal punishment. 15 PKPS 49.

c. The Ministry of Justice and the Provincial Courts

        Until 1896 the Ministry of Justice exercised control
only over the Bangkok courts. No sweeping reform of the
provincial courts had been made when the Bangkok courts
were restructured from 1892 to 1896. Indeed, very few
changes of any kind had been made in the provincial court
system to that time. With the transformation of the traditional
bureaucracy, however, the control which the three great
ministries had exercised over their respective geographical
regions was eventually removed. As a consequence, the court
system which they had administered together with the provincial
governor and provincial council had also to be changed.
Mahatthai and nakhonban were left with temporary authority
over the judiciary outside of the capital, but meaningful
centralized control would not be asserted until the provincial
courts underwent a restructuring similar to that of the Bangkok
courts from 1892 to 1896.

On January 2, 1896 a new Law of the Provincial Courts was promulgated which reorganized the workings of the entire Thai judiciary at the provincial level, and required cooperation in its supervision among the ministries of Justice, nakhǫnban, and mahatthai. 15 PKPS 54. Three judicial levels were established: (1) monthon courts, corresponding to the regional administrative unit, would be administered by one athibǫdi, or chief judge, and at least two other judges. These officials would conduct the trials and render verdicts; (2) müang courts, corresponding to the provincial administrative unit, would be staffed in the same manner as the monthon courts; (3) khwaeng courts, sub-units of the müang, would be administered by only one judge. (Clauses 4 and 7). In the region (monthon) of the capital itself, only the müang and khwaeng courts were to be established, since the Royal Appeals Court already fulfilled the function of a monthon court. (Clause 4).

Three classes of judges were created under the new law, each with a different jurisdictional authority. The third class judges were empowered to decide all punishable offenses involving penalties up to one month imprisonment or a fifty baht fine, and all civil cases involving amounts up to fifty baht. (Clause 12). The jurisdiction of the second class judges was limited to punishable offenses involving penalties of up to three months, one hundred baht, or thirty strokes with a rattan stick, and civil cases of up to one hundred baht. (Clause 13). The first class judges had jurisdiction over punishable offenses of six months, two hundred baht, or fifty strokes, and civil cases involving up to two hundred baht. (Clause 14). The jurisdiction of the khwaeng and müang courts was then limited to the jurisdictional authority of the judge who presided. In addition, the müang judges sitting en banc could hear cases exceeding their individual jurisdictional powers: civil cases of up to five thousand baht and criminal cases involving any prison term, beating, or fine of five thousand baht or less. (Clauses 16 and 17). Appeals from judgements of both the khwaeng and müang courts went to the monthon court, which also exercised original jurisdiction over any violation of statutory law. Appeals from the monthon court went directly to the appellate courts of the capital. (Clause 20).

The chief judges, or athibǫdi, were given a major role

in the supervision of the provincial court system, but their work could be subjected to the control of the provincial administrators. The power of the athibǫdi in the müang court, for example, was limited by the approval of the highest official in the müang. (Clause 21). In this way, the newly constituted court system was prevented from becoming too powerful and independent as a political force in the provinces.

The establishment and supervision of the new provincial court system was an interesting study in the exercise of royal power, both judicial and political. It was believed by the king and by his Adviser-General, Rolin-Jacquemyns, that the provincial judges and lawyers lacked the legal knowledge and perhaps the political authority necessary to transform the judiciary unassisted. For this reason, the king on September 21, 1896 established a group of Special Commissioners (khaa luang phiset) and authorized them to reorganize the local courts. 15 PKPS 144.[15] There were to be five Special Commissioners in all. Three were permanent appointees, and of those three at least one was usually a westerner.[16] An additional Commissioner was to be chosen by the Minister of the Interior from the locality in which the group was operating at any given time; and the fifth member of the group was to be the chief administrator of the monthon itself, the khaa luang thesaphiban.

The Special Commissioners, under the authority of the Ministers of Justice and the Interior, were to order and ensure compliance with the Law of the Provincial Courts of January 2, 1896. They were to report to the Minister of the Interior alone, however, for at this time he still had primary responsibility for the judiciary in the provinces. The Special Commissioners were to visit courts, observe trials, check the court records, test the judges' knowledge of the law, and record their recommendations for improvement. They were also empowered to conduct trials themselves, if necessary, either as a group or singly. Decisions in such cases were not to be appealed through the normal channels, but were to go directly to the king. This particular function of the Special Commissioners was expanded by a proclamation of December 12, 1896, 15 PKPS 277, in which two more Special Commissioners were appointed by the king for the specific purpose

of relieving the backlog of cases in each region where the
Commissioners worked. The two appointees, however, were
not given the general administrative powers of the original five.

Through the work of the Special Commissioners, one
monthon after another was added to the list of regions where
the Law of the Provincial Courts had been implemented.
Between June 1897 and November 1898, eleven monthon had
been incorporated into the centrally administered system.
On April 27, 1908 the Northeast monthon and the monthon of
Udorn were also brought under the supervision of the Special
Commissioners. 22 PKPS 159; 22 PKPS 160. In this way the
personal agents of the ministers of the Interior and of Justice,
with the authority of the king and the advice of foreign legal
experts, established a coherent and centralized judicial
structure throughout the country.

On April 5, 1908 King Chulalongkorn promulgated a
new Law of the Courts of Justice by which all courts except
the dika court of royal review were brought under the authority
of the Ministry of Justice. 22 PKPS 238.[17] By this enactment
the powers and responsibilities of the Minister of Justice were
increased from a local to a nationwide scale, and the supervision of the Thai judiciary was finally removed from the control of any other agency or department not specially equipped
to deal with judicial matters. The enlarged scope of the Justice
Minister's responsibilities may be reflected in the fact that a
new Assistant to the Minister of Justice was soon established
in order to help with the added work load. 23 PKPS 32
(July 12, 1909).

The court structure established in the Law of the
Provincial Courts of January 2, 1896 was reaffirmed in the new
Law of the Courts of Justice of 1908, although the jurisdiction
of each of the courts was slightly increased and the classes of
provincial judges reduced from three to two. Judges of the
second class had jurisdiction over minor offenses with penalties
not exceeding one month imprisonment, two hundred baht or,
in the case of juveniles, beatings of twenty strokes, and over
civil cases involving two hundred baht or less. (Clause 22).
Judges of the first class could decide punishable offenses with
penalties not exceeding six months or one thousand baht

and civil cases involving one thousand baht or less. (Clause 23).
The jurisdiction of the khwaeng and müang courts, as before,
was limited to the jurisdictional powers of the judge presiding,
but the müang court judges sitting en banc were empowered to
decide civil cases involving up to ten thousand baht and punishable offenses with penalties not exceeding ten years imprisonment, ten thousand baht, or beatings of thirty strokes. (Clauses
25 and 26).

The monthon court again was to exercise original
jurisdiction over any case involving a statutory infraction as
well as appeals from judgements of the khwaeng and müang
courts. (Clause 27). On December 11, 1909, however, the
king issued a proclamation stripping the monthon court of its
appellate function and of most of its judges as well. Whereas
the appellate function under the 1908 law had been shared by
the monthon court and the courts of the Special Commissioners
in Bangkok, now this function was given over entirely to the
latter (unless the Minister of Justice gave special permission
for the monthon court to hear the appeal). 23 PKPS 194.
Appeals from the judgements of the Special Commissioners
were to be sent directly by dika petition to the king. The
Appeals Court in Bangkok, which had formerly reviewed
decisions of the monthon court, was thus removed from the
provincial appellate process.

The 1908 Law of the Courts of Justice represented
the culmination of a long process of assimilation and reform
begun in the earliest years of King Chulalongkorn's reign.
All of Thailand's courts except the dika court were now supervised by one minister who was directly accountable to the king.
By 1912, two years after the death of King Chulalongkorn, even
the dika court was brought under the authority of the Ministry
of Justice. The chaos and confusion of the old system was, at
least in theory, brought to an end, and the judicial structure
was reshaped in a manner which allowed it to administer
effectively the new laws and procedures which the king wished
to enact.

3. New Laws and Procedures for the Thai Judiciary

Concurrent with King Chulalongkorn's restructuring of the Thai court system was an equally thorough revision and restatement of the procedures which the courts were to follow. It is beyond the scope of this study to undertake an analysis of all such changes in the civil and criminal laws and procedures. As they affect the important issues of law and kingship, they will be dealt with later in this chapter and in the following chapter. A description of the reorganization of the Thai judiciary would not be complete, however, without brief mention of a few of the most important changes in procedural and substantive law which accompanied the judicial reorganization.

Adjustments in the rules of evidence dated back to the earliest days of King Chulalongkorn's reign. Later, on April 1, 1895, a royal edict set forth new and elaborate evidentiary rules together with charts and tables showing which of the traditional laws were eliminated or retained. 14 PKPS 225. These rules were applied first in the Bangkok courts and then, to an increasing extent, in the provincial courts which became incorporated into the central system.

Civil procedure came to be controlled by a royal edict of November 15, 1896, which proclaimed a set of provisional rules to be followed until the committee in charge of revising the laws had prepared a complete new code. 15 PKPS 157.[18] This edict was followed by a proclamation on November 29, 1898 specifying the old laws which were replaced or amended by its provisions. 16 PKPS 423. In 1908 the new code of civil procedure was promulgated by royal edict, defining in elaborate detail such matters as jurisdiction of the court over the defendant, procedures to be followed in ordinary and in petty cases, requirements and procedures for appeals, the role of counsel, the appointment of special masters, offenses against the status and power of the court, and the assessment of costs. 22 PKPS 254. With this new code, Thai civil procedure took on an unprecedented degree of detail and precision, set forth in a form readily understandable to most western observers.

The law of punishable offenses underwent an analogous revision and restatement. On April 27, 1896, a royal edict established a provisional procedural law for all cases involving punishments imposed by the government. 15 PKPS 106. This procedure was to be followed until final codification was completed. On June 1, 1908 the new code of substantive "criminal" law was promulgated, containing significant provisions dealing with such matters as crimes against the king and the country, internal and external threats to the nation's security, crimes against diplomats and foreign relations, offenses against government officials, misuse of official position, obstruction of justice, and crimes against religion. 22 PKPS 1.[19] Certain of these provisions will be considered later in this study.

In a preface to the new criminal code in 1908, the king provided a fitting summary of his accomplishments in the area of judicial reform. Since ancient times, the king observed, the Thai monarch had defended and interpreted the thammasat as the basis for the administration of all laws in the nation. Whenever legal matters arose which could not be resolved easily by reference to the thammasat or to Thai customs, then the king would enact laws to deal with such issues. But with the passage of time and the change of conditions, such laws had proliferated and become confused and difficult to apply in the courts of the land. When such situations arose it was customary for the king, together with his advisers and the lukkhun legal experts, to revise and reform the laws.

The king had undertaken the present revision of the law of punishable offenses for these very reasons. The last revision of the laws had occurred more than a century before, and in the interim they had become outmoded and self-contra-dictory. In addition, the king pointed out, the unequal treaties with the western countries had provided another incentive to reform Thai law. Extraterritoriality required the application of many different bodies of law within Thailand itself, and as a result there was much uncertainty and confusion in dealings with aliens. All countries like Thailand, which had agreed to the establishment of extraterritorial courts, had subsequently desired to put an end to them and to make their own laws applicable to all people within their boundaries.

For this reason, concluded the king, he had chosen to follow the example of Japan, which was the first country to solve this difficult problem. By commissioning foreign legal experts to work together with local officials, Japan had revised its legal system so that the laws would resemble those of the western countries and would be administered in modern courts of justice throughout the land. Foreign nations had been willing to abolish their extraterritorial courts when they saw that order had been brought to Japan's judiciary. Similarly, foreign legal experts had been brought by the king into Thailand and a committee established to revise the Thai laws. It was clearly the expectation of King Chulalongkorn that this process of revision, together with the reorganization of the Thai courts, would lead directly to the end of extraterritoriality in Thailand and a recovery of her full rights of sovereignty.

B. Implications of the Change

King Chulalongkorn himself had described the Tahi judiciary as a rotten and leaking ship and had set about the task of building a new vessel to replace it. In his transformation of the judicial system, the king stated several different reasons why this monumental undertaking was necessary, reasons which have already been described and discussed. Beyond the commonly articulated reasons and purposes of the king, his advisers, and his ministers, however, the changes in the judicial function brought other important modifications to the traditional concepts of law and kingship. These changes may be grouped into four different categories: (1) the unification of the administration of justice and the extension of control by the central government through its centralized judiciary; (2) a growing distinction between civil and criminal law and a clearer articulation of the role of the public prosecutor; (3) a new theory of the role of the appellate courts and an end to personal liability of the trial judge upon appeal; (4) modification of the direct involvement of the king in the judicial process.

1. Unification and Extension of the Centralized Judiciary

The judicial system which King Chulalongkorn inherited had been characterized by a two-fold division in the administration of justice. A judiciary which may once have been unified under the authority of the Brahmin legal advisers, the lukkhun, had over the years been fragmented and scattered among the various ministries and departments. The trial process itself was divided between the judge who conducted the trial and the lukkhun who rendered the substantive decisions. In such a system it was impossible to assert any continuous or meaningful form of central control. The king could not rely upon the courts to enforce honest government, to combat crime and disorder in the provinces, or to implement new policies and laws which the government in Bangkok might choose to enact. The system was too slow, too complex, too expensive, too susceptible to the influence of money and political influence at its various stages and levels. The average citizen probably saw the judicial system as a hazard and a threat to his life and property, rather than as a forum for the vindication of his rights or the enforcement of just government enactments.

The changes effected by King Chulalongkorn resulted in a simplification and a unification of the Thai judiciary. Ultimately, all courts were to fall under the authority of the Minister of Justice who was responsible directly to the king. The number of courts was greatly reduced and their juris - dictional powers clearly articulated. The function of the lukkhun was eliminated, and all judicial decisions were made in the same forum which had heard the case. Not only the structure, but the procedure of the Thai courts was clarified and made applicable in the same manner throughout the entire country. The king was able to control this newly centralized system at all levels both through his Special Commissioners, who acted as observers, teachers, and magistrates, and through his Minister of Justice, who appointed judges in all courts from the khwaeng level to the highest appellate court. The only important exception to this general extension of the central judicial power was the Muslim area in the far South. Just as it had been granted a special degree of legislative independence, so it was permitted to apply traditional Islamic law, administered by Islamic judges, in cases involving family law and inheritance which were governed by religious rules, where the defendant alone or both the litigants were Islam. 18 PKPS 197 (Paragraph 32).

It is not certain that the average Thai citizen saw the reformed judiciary under King Rama V as any less menacing or complex than the old system. Nor is it clear that the judiciary was administered with restraint and understanding by the officers of the Ministry of Justice at all levels. It cannot be doubted, however, that the king had succeeded in creating an institution more responsive to his own wishes and policies, and better equipped to implement his enactments and to increase his capacity to rule throughout the country. In this respect, the judicial power of the king reached a level which had never before been attained by any of his predecessors.

2. The Distinction between Civil and
   Criminal Law

Under traditional Thai law, no clear line was drawn
between suits which many other legal systems would distinguish
as civil and criminal. Most lawsuits required the participation
of two private litigants and, with the exception of certain
particularly grave offenses, failure of the victim to come
forward as plaintiff meant that the perpetrator of a wrongful
act could escape punishment.[20] It is the opinion of one
commentator that the courts were used primarily for the
litigation of punishable offenses and that purely civil suits,
suits not involving the punishment of the defendant, were
rarely brought.[21] The legal reforms of King Chulalongkorn
not only sharpened the distinction between punishable and non-
punishable causes of action, but also defined with greater
precision the role which the prosecutor was to play in the
enforcement of the law.

Several statutes enacted under King Chulalongkorn
undertook to distinguish civil cases from those arising out of
behavior directly injurious to the state. In the provisional
civil procedure edict of 1896, 15 PKPS 157, civil cases were
defined as those in which no criminal punishment was requested
and the remedy sought was a money judgement. (Clause 4).
This description, however, was amended in a proclamation of
March 7, 1900. 17 PKPS 197. The later definition included
both those cases in which no criminal punishment was requested, and those in which criminal punishment was requested
together with other relief, where the criminal punishment was
not an "important" matter under the law. No explanation of
the word "important" was offered. The 1900 definition of civil
cases significantly omitted the requirement that the case be
susceptible to settlement by a money judgement, and would
therefore appear to include suits requesting relief in the form
of mandatory decrees, such as court ordered injunctions and
orders of specific performance. The category of "civil" suits
thus grew broad enough to cover all cases whose major aspects
were not criminal in nature.

In the criminal area, too, there were some changes

which suggested that the injured party was beginning to play a role more closely akin to that of complainant, while the prosecutor as representative of the state became the real plaintiff. On July 18, 1903, for example, it was ordered that no court costs should be assessed at trial whenever an injured party alleged some punishable offense but requested no money judgement. The financial burden of bringing such suits apparently was to fall either on the state or on the defendant but not upon the victim as plaintiff. 19 PKPS 38. In the criminal code of 1908, 22 PKPS 1, it was provided that the plaintiff could file two suits against the defendant, one criminal in nature requesting that a punishment be imposed, and the other civil in nature requesting that the defendant make the plaintiff whole. A civil suit might be brought, for example, to regain possession of stolen property. If, however, the plaintiff neglected to file any civil action, the court was nevertheless obliged to return wrongfully acquired property to its proper owner if he or she could be ascertained. (Clauses 87-96). The criminal action would normally precede the civil action. If it happened that the civil suit was brought before the criminal suit then, under the civil procedure edict of 1908, 22 PKPS 254, the civil action was to be suspended whenever it appeared that the disposition of the related criminal matter might affect the judgement of the civil court. The judge in such cases was to order that the criminal matter be resolved before litigation could proceed in the related civil suit. (Clause 41).

As these distinctions between civil and criminal litigation gradually developed, the role of the prosecutor also became increasingly prominent. In the provisional law of criminal procedure, enacted April 27, 1896, it was provided that the state should act as plaintiff in certain criminal offenses whenever the injured party did not appear in court to bring suit, or whenever he should bring suit but fail for any reason to pursue the litigation. Among the criminal offenses listed under this provision were serious violations such as murder, rape, larceny, and crimes against religion. 15 PKPS 106 (Clause 7). As the role of the prosecutor in criminal trials was gradually enlarged, so was his presence in all jurisdictions throughout the country. In the 1896 Law of the Provincial Courts, it was required that the provincial governor and the chief judge in each province appoint a prosecutor and a substitute prosecutor respectively. 15 PKPS 54 (Clauses 25 and 26). In this way, the prosecution of serious crimes throughout the country was assured, even when the victim for one reason or another should fail to bring suit.

The roles of the prosecutor and the police were differentiated in a royal edict of April 1, 1897. Here it was stated that the preparation of a case against a criminal defendant was the work of the prosecutor and not the police. The investigator's office of the nakhọnban ministry was abolished and its work transferred to the prosecutor's office in the Ministry of Justice. The investigation, prosecution, and punishment of the criminal offender were thus brought together under the authority of the Justice Ministry. 16 PKPS 7. This edict was significant not only because it gave the Ministry of Justice a new and important respoonsibility which had formerly belonged to nakhọnban, but also because it enabled the Ministry of Justice to implement more effectively the policies of the central government in the suppression of crime.

The final and most elaborate statement of the prosecutor's function came in the Law of the Courts of Justice, 1908. Under this statute each court in the Ministry of Justice was to be provided with a prosecutor acting as the government's lawyer. The duties of the prosecutor in this capacity included not only civil litigation in which the government was a party, but all offenses punishable under law. The role of the prosecutor was thus extended to include criminal suits in which a plaintiff had already appeared to bring charges against the defendant. In such cases it was evidently possible for the prosecutor to join with the plaintiff in an action against the criminal defendant. If the original plaintiff should drop out of the suit for any reason, the prosecutor could proceed with the litigation alone. 22 PKPS 238 (Clauses 33-35).

By 1908 the prosecutor's role had expanded to the point where, in all courts under the Ministry of Justice, he could initiate or join in any criminal action. Although the injured party retained his or her traditional right to appear as a plaintiff in such cases, the prosecutor could perform his function concurrently with the victim. By this means, the central government was assured that its interests would be represented in all courts throughout the country, and that criminal actions would be vigorously prosecuted whenever they came to the attention of the prosecutor. The overlapping character of civil and criminal types of litigation would not, therefore, impede the government in seeing its laws and policies enforced in the courts of the Ministry of Justice.

3. Appeals

Under the traditional system of law which prevailed before the reign of King Rama V, an appeal was, in effect, a criminal suit directed by the losing party against the trial judge or one of the witnesses. Because of the traditional belief that justice sprang from the pervasive influence of thamma, the laws of moral truth, it was thought that the rightful party in a lawsuit would triumph unless the judge had violated the law or a witness had perjured himself. For this reason, the party who lost at the trial level, if he chose to appeal, had to allege that either the judge or a witness had broken the law and obstructed the workings of moral truth. If the appellant succeeded in proving such allegations, then the judge or witness was punished and the case was retried. If the appellant failed, then he himself was punished because he had improperly accused others of error when it was actually he who was in the wrong.[22] The fear of losing the case on appeal and subjecting oneself to punishment as a result, together with the expense of the appeals process, discouraged most litigants from seeking review of an adverse judgement.[23]

This concept of the appellate function was fundamentally changed during King Chulalongkorn's reign, and it is fitting that Prince Phitchit Prichakǫn helped to institute the change. Prince Phitchit, in his essay on justice, had emphasized the relationship between justice in the courts of law and the rules of thamma in the moral universe. This point of view accorded well with the traditional concept of an appeal as a criminal action directed against a judge or witness who had allegedly violated the sacred law and had thereby wronged an innocent party. As Minister of Justice, however, on November 18, 1894, Prince Phitchit issued an order which ended the liability of the trial judge who was reversed on appeal. 14 PKPS 199. Prior to that time the trial judge was commonly charged four percent of the amount in controversy plus court costs if his decision was reversed. Prince Phitchit ordered, however, that the appellate court should no longer consider the trial judge a party in the appeal nor should he be required to pay anything upon reversal. The only exception to this rule arose when the judge was accused of some illegal activity, such as the acceptance of a bribe, in which case he did in fact appear before the appellate court as a defendant.

Prince Phitchit's justification for this change was a practical one. He had observed that many trial judges delayed the delivery of their verdicts because of their fear that the losing party would appeal the decision and subject them to liability in a higher court. This was one of the reasons that the trial dockets were filled with cases awaiting decision. Since nothing in the traditional law texts required that the trial judge be considered a defendant on appeal, Prince Phitchit felt that the older approach to appeals should be abandoned. This practical justification, however, had profound theoretical implications. Prince Phitchit had clearly moved away from a concept of the courts as instruments for effectuating the absolute rules of thamma, and had recognized that the workings of the moral laws of nature and the written laws of man might in reality be very different things.

With this fundamental change in the concept of the appellate function, the rules regarding appeals took on a greater sophistication. On December 11, 1895, a general prohibition was imposed upon all interlocutory appeals. This new rule, which had first been tested in the porisapha courts of Bangkok, was found necessary to prevent the delays and interruptions which resulted from appeals raised throughout the trial process. Although interlocutory review of rulings by the trial judge was forbidden, objections during the trial were to be recorded and preserved for the appellate court after a final verdict was rendered. 15 PKPS 24.

Another abuse was corrected on December 8, 1902,

when the Minister of Justice ordered that the losing party at
trial be given fifteen days in which to decide whether or not to
appeal. The trial judge was thereby prevented from forcing
the losing party to indicate his intentions immediately after the
announcement of the verdict. Too many litigants, it was found,
had been bound in haste either to accept an unjust verdict or
else to wage a frivolous appeal. 18 PKPS 483. Finally, on
March 24, 1904, a royal edict placed strict limits on the
ability of any party to appeal his case beyond the first appellate
level. It was decreed that, unless two conditions were met,
no criminal or civil case could be appealed beyond the first
level if it involved a judgement not exceeding two chang (160
baht) and was affirmed by the first appeals court or modified
in only a minor way. The two conditions, intended to ensure
that only worthy appeals would be pursued, were (1) the trial
judge or the judge of the first appellate court had granted
permission for further appeal because the case presented an
important issue; or (2) a minister, a monthon commissioner,
the head of the prosecutor's department, or two attorneys,
had signed a statement that the appeal was in fact worthy of
further consideration. 19 PKPS 114.

These modifications of the appellate function suggest
fundamental changes in the concept of law and the function of
government in relation to the law. The government, as a
servant of the king, was no longer a mere custodian of the
sacred law nor an interpreter of absolute moral truths in the
trial courts of the land. If this were still the case, then it
would be entirely proper that the errors of the trial judge
should be punishable as violations of the sacred law. Instead,
the judiciary had become an organ for the interpretation of man-
made laws, not absolute moral truths, and in such interpreta-
tions honest men might reasonably differ. When disagreements
arose, they were to be handled in an orderly way, without
obstructing the procedures of the trial court and without expos-
ing the trial judge to the hazards of personal liability. Since
the losing party at trial was no longer deterred from appeals
by fear for his own personal safety, moreover, a new and more
rational screening process had to be devised. For this reason,
strict preconditions were imposed upon all appeals after an
initial and unsuccessful review at the first appellate level.
Both the trial courts and the appellate courts were thus enabled

to function without obstruction and without a flood of frivolous cases; and at the same time all litigants were assured of the right to a meaningful review of the trial itself by at least one appellate court.

4. Exercise of the Judicial Powers of
the King

Since the earliest days of the patriarchal monarchy one of the primary judicial functions of the Thai king had been the hearing of petitions from the people. The king was an ultimate court of review, deciding appeals for clemency and for other forms of personal intervention in all cases which came to him by royal, or dika, appeal. With the reorganization of the Thai judiciary under King Chulalongkorn, however, the king's personal role in the appellate process grew more sporadic and indirect. Although his power over the conduct of the judiciary had increased greatly, his active participation in its ordinary functions had become less intense.

In 1874 the king had required that the athibodi in each department screen those cases which would otherwise have gone directly to the king on appeal. This was the first of many attempts to diminish the number of cases brought for royal review and to establish other bodies which would assist the king in his appellate function. The old patriarchal custom of personal review by the king still persisted, however, as may be seen in a proclamation of 1884 which described the proper procedure for forming lines at the palace door on specified days of the month in order to present petitions to the king. 10 PKPS 140. The king's attempts to delegate his dika review function -- to the various departmental athibodi, to the mae kong, to the dika court composed of his own relatives -- had not achieved any notable success during the early years of his reign. It was apparent that the king could not entrust his traditional power of ultimate review to any other group or individual until the entire judicial system was reorganized. The practice of dika review by the king could not be reformed and revitalized without the assistance of a restructured court system with its own appellate mechanism and filtering apparatus.

A second form of personal intervention by the traditional monarch in the Thai judicial process had been his supervision of violent crimes and murders, and his power to impose the death sentence on defendants found guilty of such crimes. King Chulalongkorn stated that the officials of nakhọnban would consult with the king before trying such cases, and frequently the king would give them his personal authority to proceed and to report directly to him.24 The purpose of this practice was to prevent other influences from obstructing the trial and punishment of criminals who disrupted the peace and order of the kingdom. Traditionally the king also reserved for himself or for a specially designated agent the power to impose the death sentence. This custom was apparently rooted in the Buddhist reverence for life and an unwillingness to permit anyone except the "Lord of Life" himself to order the death even of a convicted murderer.

The monarch's role in connection with violent crimes gradually changed because of the judicial reforms enacted under King Chulalongkorn. In the Law of the Provincial Courts of 1896, it was required that the king's permission be obtained before any of the three provincial courts could impose a sentence involving either the death penalty or the confiscation of the defendant's property as punishment for his misdeeds. Only after the king's approval was obtained could such a punishment be carried out. 15 PKPS 54 (Clause 19). This rule was modified in the provisional procedural law for punishable offenses enacted April 27, 1896. There it was provided that the three most serious forms of punishment -- the death sentence, the confiscation of the defendant's property, and life imprisonment-- must first be approved by the Appeals Court. After such approval, the Minister of Justice was required to present these cases to the king. 15 PKPS 106 (Clauses 38-39). The king thus added one more appellate screen between the sentence of the trial court and his personal review. At the same time, however, he increased the number of cases in which a special review was required by including sentences of life imprisonment with the original two categories of capital punishment and confiscation of the defendant's property.

While describing the particular criminal sentences which required special review, the king also made it clear that other lesser forms of punishment could be imposed directly by the local authorities. In a proclamation of October 21, 1896 the king observed that many criminal cases had formerly been submitted to him for determining the sentence appropriate to a given crime. This was no longer necessary, announced the king, for the Law of the Provincial Courts and the new civil and criminal procedural laws now empowered the local courts to impose sentences on defendants whom they had tried and found guilty. By consulting the royal laws of punishments, the provincial courts were to sentence the defendants themselves. 15 PKPS 232. By a proclamation of March 10, 1897, this power was granted to the Bangkok courts as well. 15 PKPS 250.

Finally, in the Criminal Code of 1908, it was required that the approval of the king be obtained before imposition of the death penalty. 22 PKPS 1 (Clause 14). No mention was made of obtaining the king's approval in cases involving life imprisonment or the confiscation of the defendant's property, and it may be inferred from this omission that such sentences were now within the powers of the lower courts. The traditional function of the king in supervising violent crimes throughout the kingdom had been delegated by and large to the newly restruc- tured court system and to the prosecutors in each of the courts. Only the highest function of the traditional "Lord of Life" was still exercised directly by the king himself in the imposition of the death sentence.

In a similar manner, the role of the king in hearing petitions for royal review was modified by the later reforms of King Chulalongkorn. In the proclamation establishing a Ministry of Justice in 1892 the king indicated that he would no longer receive all petitions of the people indiscriminately. Rather, the Royal Appeals Court was to decide all pending dika cases, and in the future the king would hear only four types of cases: (1) alleged errors of the Royal Appeals Court, (2) alleged errors of the People's Appeals Court, (3) appeals directed against the ministry heads, (4) other matters which were worthy of the king's personal attention. 13 PKPS 74 (Paragraph 6).

The king also succeeded in establishing a body able to assist him with those cases which did reach him on appeal.

The old and ineffective dika court was revitalized by the
creation of a new committee of five legal specialists, which
was to operate concurrently in the hearing of dika suits. This
committee, whose members included Prince Phitchit Prichakǫn
and the Belgian legal expert, R.J. Kirkpatrick, was to decide
dika cases independently of the older group. When the two
bodies arrived at different results, then the total number of
votes in both groups were to be added together to reach a
decision. 16 PKPS 374 (May 29, 1898). At last the king
seemed to have found a viable way to delegate to others the
power of ultimate review.

In the later years of King Chulalongkorn's reign,
further restrictions were imposed upon those cases which
could be submitted for dika review. On May 5, 1898, a royal
proclamation announced the types of civil and criminal suits
which were deemed appropriate. Generally cases could be
brought before the dika court if they involved judgements by
the lower courts in excess of two chang or six months imprisonment. No case which failed to meet these conditions could be
raised unless (1) the trial judge or appellate judge permitted
a dika appeal because he believed the matter to be of special
importance, or (2) any minister or monthon commissioner, the
head of the prosecutor's department, or any two attorneys,
attested to the propriety of a dika appeal in the particular
case. 16 PKPS 357. Five years later, on February 2, 1903,
the Minister of Justice took further steps to prevent time from
being wasted on cases unworthy of dika review. He ordered
that no court should permit a dika appeal for any case which
failed to meet the two chang or six month limitation. Litigants
in such cases were required personally to request permission
for a special exception from the dika court itself. 18 PKPS 543.
By a royal edict on March 24, 1904 the restrictions upon cases
qualifying for dika review were further tightened. No dika
appeal was permitted in civil or criminal cases where the
judgement did not exceed five chang and the appellate court
had affirmed the trial court's decision or made only minor
revisions, unless, as before, (1) the trial judge or appellate
judge believed the matter to be of special importance, or (2)
any minister or monthon commissioner, the head of the
prosecutor's department, or any two attorneys attested to the
propriety of a dika appeal in the particular case. 19 PKPS 114
(Clause 2).

Finally, in the major enactments of 1908, the nature
and function of the dika appellate review were set forth with
clarity. In the Law of the Courts of Justice of 1908, a dika
court was formally established as the highest court of appeals.
It was to be presided over by a group of judges whose numbers
depended upon the wishes of the king, although a panel of three
judges was sufficient to hear and decide cases in the name of
the court. 22 PKPS 238 (Clause 6). By retaining the power to
appoint additional judges at any time, the king could control
the composition and judicial philosophy of the court. Although
the statute formally delegated to the court the complete power
to decide dika appeals, it also provided that the court could
request the advice of the king before reaching its decision. By
this means, and by the king's power of appointment, it may be
surmised that the king retained some influence over the
decisions of the dika court, particularly in important lawsuits,
while divesting himself of the burdensome task of deciding all
dika appeals.

The Law of the Courts of Justice defined those cases
which could be appealed to the dika level as (1) appeals from
decisions of the Appeals Court, or (2) suits against ministry
officials relating to the performance of their official duties,
when such cases could not be brought in other courts.
(Clause 5). In the Civil Procedure edict of 1908 the jurisdiction of the dika court over civil suits was identical to that
in the earlier edict of March 24, 1904 (page
except that cases involving mandatory court decrees could
also be appealed to the dika court even where the minimum
jurisdictional amount of five chang (four hundred baht) was not
at stake. 22 PKPS 254 (Clause 144).

To summarize, then, the dika function of the king was
by 1908 delegated in its entirety to the dika court over which
the king nevertheless retained a significant influence in
important cases. The dika process itself was modified by
jurisdictional limitations upon the types of cases which could
be raised for appeal in the highest court. In these two ways,
the personal role of the patriarchal kings in hearing cases
brought before them by the people was replaced by a more
westernized and "rationalized" concept of appellate review.

In addition, the king's traditional supervisory role in cases involving violent crimes had been delegated entirely to the courts, to the Minister of Justice, and to the prosecutor's office. The king retained only the power to impose the death sentence upon persons convicted of capital crimes. As for the suppression of outlaws and the preservation of peace and order in the kingdom, the king had actually strengthened his powers in this respect by delegating them to government officials in the capital and in the provinces. By applying the newly revised laws and procedures in the newly restructured court system, these officials, in the name of the king, were able to exert an unprecedented degree of control over the judicial function. King Chulalongkorn, in his reformation of the Thai judiciary, had vastly increased the traditional powers of the king to implement new policies and laws in Bangkok and the provinces. He had by this same process taken the first successful step toward his primary foreign policy objective of treaty revision and the abolition of the extraterritorial courts.

NOTES

1. Wales, pp. 178-179.

2. Chompunut Nakiraks, "Bot bat khǫng thi prüksa chao
    tang prathet nai ratchasamai phrabat somdet phra
    čhunlačhǫmklao čhaoyuhua p.s. 2411-p.s. 2453
    [The role of Foreign Advisers During the Reign of
    Rama V from 1868-1910]," M.A. thesis (Chula-
    longkorn University, Bangkok, 1970), pp. 65-66,
    citing papers of Rolin-Jacquemyns on file at Fine Arts
    Department, Ministry of Education, Bangkok. For a
    general account of Rolin-Jacquemyns' career in
    Thailand and those of the other Belgian advisers he
    recruited for the Thai government, see Christian de
    Saint-Hubert, "Rolin-Jacquemyns (Chao Phya Aphay
    Raja) and the Belgian Legal Advisers in Siam at the
    Turn of the Century," Siam Society Journal, 53, pt. 2
    (1965), pp. 181-190.

3. See King Chulalongkorn, Phraratchadamrat song
    thalaeng..., pp. 15-33.

4. Prince Damrong Rachanuphap states that the department
    was composed of twelve men. Laksana kan pokkhrǫng
    ..., p. 50.

5. Prince Ratburi Direkrit, in describing the steps of
    litigation, does not mention the examination of the
    preliminary hearing record by the lukkhun, a step
    which is included in Prince Damrong's more detailed
    account, Laksana kan pokkrǫng..., pp. 50-51. The
    description by Prince Ratburi Direkrit is from
    Phraratchabanyat nai patyuban lem 1 [Royal Edicts
    in the Present Day, Vol. 1] (Bangkok 1901),
    pp. 153-154, as quoted in Thanin Kraiwichian, Kan
    patirup rabop kotmai lae kan san nai ratchasamai
    phrabatsomdet phračhunlačhǫmklao čhaoyuhua

phrapiyamaharat [Transformation of the Legal
System and the Judiciary During the Reign of King
Chulalongkorn] (Bangkok 1968), p. 44.

6.   This theory was suggested by King Chulalongkorn in
Phraratchadamrat song thalaeng..., pp. 19-20.

7.   Phra Wǫraphakphibun, p. 110, referring to laksana
aya luang [Law of Offenses Against the Government],
Clause 45.

8.   King Chulalongkorn, Phraratchadamrat song thalaeng
..., pp. 21-22; Wales, p. 184; Prince Damrong,
Laksana kan pokkhrǫng..., p. 52. The administration
of justice in the provinces during the period before
King Chulalongkorn's reign is a subject of some uncertainty. Even this brief summary, therefore, is
offered as a tentative and by no means a conclusive
description.

9.   See Wyatt, Politics of Reform..., p. 52.

10.   Wyatt, Politics of Reform..., p. 52, fn. 36. Decree of
March 10, 1875 cited by Professor Wyatt was unavail-
able.

11.   Described in King Chulalongkorn, Phraratchadamrat
song thalaeng..., p. 22.

12.   Described in King Chulalongkorn, Phraratchadamrat
song thalaeng..., pp. 29-31.

13.   King Chulalongkorn, Phraratchadamrat song thalaeng
..., p. 31.

14.   King Chulalongkorn, Phraratchadamrat song thalaeng
..., pp. 32-33.

15.   See also Chompunut Nakiraks, p. 66, regarding the
influence of Rolin-Jacquemyns; Phra Wǫraphakphibun,
p. 279.

16.   Richard Jacques Kirkpatrick, a Belgian jurist who
served as Legal Advisor to King Chulalongkorn, was

appointed September 21, 1896 to the position of Special Commissioner. 15 PKPS 148. He was replaced on May 9, 1903 by J. Stewart Black, an Englishman. 19 PKPS 12. Both men are mentioned in Tokichi Masao, "The New Penal Code of Siam," 18 Yale Law Journal 85 (December, 1908), p. 86. See Also Christian de Saint-Hubert, "Rolin-Jacquemyns...".

17. No date is provided in the Law of the Courts of Justice itself. April 5, 1908 represents the date of publication in the Ratchakitčhanubeksa (Royal Thai Government Gazette).

18. Date is again obtained from Ratchakitčhanubeksa.

19. Date obtained from Ratchakitčhanubeksa.

20. According to Prince Ratburi Direkrit, there were certain situations in which the court would proceed against a criminal defendant even when the plaintiff failed to appear. It was common for the court itself, in cases involving certain types of robberies, to assume an accusatorial role and sternly prosecute the alleged wrongdoer. This observation is from the passage by Prince Ratburi Direkrit quoted in Thanin Kraiwichian, Kan patirup rabop kotmai..., p. 44, cited in footnote 5 above.

21. Wales, p. 183. Constance M. Wilson, in her analysis of the reign of King Rama IV, suggests that most lawsuits brought at that time (1851 to 1868) concerned bandits, thieves and disturbers of the peace. "Civil" litigation was used primarily to collect debts, recover the services of escaped slaves, and to resolve inheritance disputes. Constance M. Wilson, "State and Society in the Reign of Mongkut, 1851-1868: Thailand on the Eve of Modernization," Ph. D. diss. (Cornell University, 1970), p. 412.

22. Phra Wǫraphakphibun, pp. 302-303.

23. Wales, p. 186.

24. King Chulalongkorn, Phraratchadamrat song thalaeng ..., p. 23.

CHAPTER 4

RIGHTS OF PRIVATE CITIZENS

It was perhaps a paradox that, as the Thai monarchy
reached its zenith of power under King Chulalongkorn, the
rights of private citizens also attained an unprecedented and
probably irreversible stage in their development. The king's
administrative powers could only be exercised by authorizing
other officials throughout the country to act in his name. This
delegation of responsibility took the form of royal enactments
which set forth the powers and duties of the officials under law,
both towards the king and towards the people. As a result,
the lawful behavior of government bureaucrats became less
arbitrary, less capricious, and, to a greater degree than ever
before, the people themselves acquired the power to hold these
men accountable for their actions. On a theoretical level at
least, a new set of legal rights began to develop. In most
cases these rights protected the people from unjust and arbitrary
conduct by the officials who wielded the king's new powers. But
also, to a limited extent, these rights touched on other areas
of great significance for the future: rights of speech and of
representation in the government itself.

A. Social Legislation

For the most part the social legislation of King
Chulalongkorn lies outside the scope of this study. The subject
should not, however, be passed over entirely without mention,
for it raises some important questions about the citizen's right
to equal protection under law. The legislation is significant
here because of its effect in breaking down traditional social
classifications and suggesting that the private citizen had
attained, regardless of class, certain common rights to fair
and equal treatment which were enforceable in the courts of
justice.

The Thai people had traditionally been divided into
four general classes: čhao, khunnang, phrai, and that. The

čhao were royalty, persons closely related to the king. The "declining descent rule" prevented this social classification from being retained by one family indefinitely, for each generation descended from the monarchy was assigned a lower royal rank until the distinction was lost altogether by the sixth generation.[1] The khunnang were the nobility, so designated by virtue of the number of sakdina, or dignity marks, assigned to them, which in turn represented the number of men whose services and manpower they could control.[2] The phrai were the men who owed services, either to some leader known as a munnai in the case of phrai som, or else to the king in the case of the phrai luang. In return for the services of the phrai, rendered on a yearly basis in a relationship regulated under traditional laws, the munnai offered a form of paternalistic protection to the phrai who served him. The fourth group, the that, were slaves. They could assert most of the legal rights of other citizens, but had chosen to sell their freedom under a contract whose terms could, in most cases, be redeemed when the original purchase price had been repaid.[3]

One commentator has observed that these four general classes of citizens had undergone considerable change in the first half of the nineteenth century.[4] Prior to that time the princes had become powerful through the acquisition of more phrai than their position strictly merited. Most of these phrai were phrai luang who had escaped their obligations to the king and attached themselves to a prince instead. In the early nineteenth century, however, this situation was corrected by marking all phrai with tatooes of their munnai. As the princes subsequently lost power, the nobles gained power through informal hierarchies based on new wealth brought into the country through foreign trade. Their increased wealth and status put them in a position to offer greater protection and benefits to men who gave them their services than could the traditional munnai, and in this way the old system began to break down. The phrai became more and more oppressed, finding it increasingly difficult to satisfy the demands of their beleaguered munnai, who were themselves caught between rising costs of living and diminished income. In addition, the phrai were forced to channel much of their wealth into payments to the new "tax farmers" who had bid for and obtained the position of private tax collectors for the government with the right to keep as profit all income beyond the amount they had bid.[5] It is understandable that many free men found it enticing to sell themselves and their families as slaves, not only for the purpose of acquiring money by the sale but because the tax burdens on slaves were less oppressive.

The legislation of King Chulalongkorn brought profound changes to all four classes of citizens. The royalty was greatly strengthened not only by the enormous increase in power of the king himself, but by his dependence upon his own relatives whom he appointed as advisers, legislators, ministers, and officials. The remaining three classes were also affected during this period, by King Chulalongkorn's abolition of slavery, by his restrictions on forced labor, by the implementation of a more equitable tax system, and by the enactment of universal conscription for the military. A few important points are especially worthy of mention here.

The abolition of slavery, like many of the other reforms, was an exercise in gradualism. The king extended the process of emancipation over a period of more than thirty years, partly to avoid opposition from the nobility and upper classes who might otherwise have resisted the change. The king also knew of the Russian and American problems in bringing about similar reforms and may have wished to minimize in Thailand the social turmoil which those countries had experienced.[6] The king himself cited two more justifications for the gradualist approach to emancipation when he first embarked on that course in 1874. He contended that the abolition of slavery depended not only on the promulgation of one great proclamation by the king, but upon an elimination of the root cause of slavery: namely, inequality in the payment of taxes. Slaves should not be permitted to pay lower taxes nor to rely wholly upon their masters for sustenance instead of holding regular jobs themselves. When this situation was rectified then the incentive to become a slave would be removed, and the practice would end of its own accord. In addition, the king looked to compulsory primary education as a long-term means to bring about the end of slavery. When children were well-educated and could find work without difficulty, then they themselves would not wish to become or remain slaves.[7]

King Chulalongkorn believed that slavery in Thailand, although more voluntary and less oppressive than in other countries, was nevertheless an obstacle to the attainment of real progress and well-being. 20 PKPS 24. It is likely that he was sensitive in this regard to the image of Thailand in the eyes of the western countries. If the custom of slavery in Thailand was regarded by them as backward or as a symbol of the injustice of Thailand's laws, then it was essential for purposes of national self-protection that the custom be abandoned no matter how well-entrenched it had become. For these reasons, among others, slavery was abolished in Thailand by stages. In 1874 the scheme of costs for redeeming the children of slaves was revised in such a way that any child who was then a slave would be freed automatically by the age of twenty-one. 8 PKPS 280. In 1905 the king by royal edict decreed that all children of slaves should be immediately freed (except in certain Muslim provinces where local custom was to continue in effect), that no one should henceforth be permitted to sell himself into slavery, and that those who were presently slaves should be permitted to redeem themselves at a lower monthly rate of payment. 20 PKPS 24. In 1912, less than two years after the death of King Chulalongkorn, the practice of slavery was totally abolished by his successor.

Forced labor, once the backbone of the traditional social structure, was also restricted severely and replaced by a more equitable tax system and by a nationwide military draft. To a certain degree, however, forced labor by men and animals was still permitted in order to perform in the provinces essential tasks related to the public interest. Such tasks included the capture and transport of criminals and the improvement of public works such as roads and waterways. It was required by law, however, that when a public "taking" of the labor and time of men and animals occurred, it should be compensated according to a specific rate of payment published by the king. The traditional prerogative of personal power, the right to command the services of a number of men who were the "clients" in a formal master-client hierarchy under ancient law, was therefore challenged by a new legal concept. The new concept required that such services be demanded only for the benefit of the community or the state and that they be compensated according to a scale of payments known to all. 17 PKPS

528; 17 PKPS 542.

The military draft was first enacted by royal edict on August 29, 1905, and was extended gradually to each of the monthon throughout the country. It applied for the most part to all men equally, rather than affecting only those phrai who happened to be attached to a government department whose functions were military in nature, as had previously been the case. All men between the ages of eighteen and forty were included in the sweep of the edict. (Clauses 4 and 5). The term of service was seventeen years altogether: two years of active service and fifteen years in two different types of reserve duty. (Clause 7). Certain groups remained unaffected by the draft, among them monks, college students, government officials, Chinese immigrants and their children, forest and hill tribes, and others. (Clauses 13 and 14). Although exemptions were granted on various grounds of necessity, two provisions in particular revealed the king's interest in encouraging commerce and promoting lucrative sources of government revenue: exemptions from the military draft were extended to farmers who did a great deal of business and paid a specified tax to the government, and to the heads of companies which paid a certain amount in government revenues. (Clause 13). The edict as a whole suggested a new equality in the obligation owed by each citizen under law. This egalitarian theory was not, however, to override compelling interests such as agriculture, commerce, and tax revenues for the government. Also, a special status was granted in this scheme to royalty and to the educated. Royalty, from the rank of mǫm čhao upwards, were to be commissioned as officers or cadets. Persons who had passed the higher education test were to act as teachers in the military for a period of one year, at the end of which time their military service was to end. 20 PKPS 302. (Clause 15).

In a brief announcement of some significance, the king, acting through the Minister of Justice, on January 14, 1906 gave the Thai judiciary a direct role in supervising the new military draft. 20 PKPS 521. He ordered that disputes as to who should be drafted or exempted should be decided by the courts of the Ministry of Justice. Apparently the private citizen had gained an enforceable right to fair treatment and to due process in his dealings with at least one administrative agency. Not only were his obligations to the government made less oppressive and distributed more fairly among the population as a whole, but the entire administrative procedure was now described by statute and reviewable in the courts of the Ministry of Justice. While it is not clear that the system actually functioned as it was set forth in the statute, the conceptual development alone is significant in so far as it reveals a new legal relationship between the citizen and the state. The demands of the state were to be reasonable and necessary, they were to be distributed in the form of obligations owed equally by nearly all citizens, and they were to be administered with fairness according to detailed rules which the Thai judiciary was empowered to review and enforce.

B. Suits Against Government Officials

The role of the courts in overseeing the fairness of the military draft was part of a tendency during the reign of King Chulalongkorn to make government officials accountable to the people. The Law of the Three Seals had also contained certain restraints upon official misbehavior. In the laksana aya luang, or Law of Offenses Against the Government, it was a punishable offense for any official to threaten injury to the people, to persecute the people, or to behave in a corrupt or dishonest manner. [8] In the laksana aya ratsadon, or Law of Offenses Against the People, it was required, among other provisions, that officials receive all suits brought by the people, that they refrain from punishment or persecution of individuals bringing suits, and that no one should beat or imprison any person without justification. [9]

It is probably fair to assume, however, that few suits based upon these laws had traditionally been brought against government officials. The judicial process was full of uncertainties and dangers and was subject at all stages to the exercise of improper influence by the party against whom such a suit might be brought. It has been observed that the munnai was the normal channel through which the various complaints of the phrai were brought to the attention of the government, [10] and it seems likely that most complaints about official mis- behavior were handled in this informal and extra-judicial manner.

It is by no means clear that the constraints of custom, the traditional deference felt toward authority and the traditional avoidance of the judiciary on the part of the people, were eliminated by legal reforms enacted during the reign of King Chulalongkorn. It is significant at least in the development of legal theory, however, that the behavior of government officials was increasingly subjected to rules and restrictions imposed upon them by law and enforceable against them by the public. Specific crimes and instances of official corruption were listed in the Criminal Code of 1908. Among these, for example, were the misappropriation of government funds, the exploitation of official position to obtain profit, the acceptance of bribes (with the penalty most severe in the case of judges), and the misuse of official position to injure another party. 22 PKPS 1 (Clauses 129-146). Presumably such suits, like other suits involving punishable offenses, could be brought against the official either by the prosecutor or by the injured party.

Certain important limitations were imposed upon the people's right to sue government officials for misbehavior in office. By an edict promulgated April 29, 1901, courts were forbidden to receive criminal suits brought by private citizens against government officials on matters involving government business unless certain preconditions were satisfied. It was required that the complainant first present to the court evidence which would be sufficient to prove the official's guilt. Only then would notice be sent to the official and to the head of his govern- ment office, but such notice would be a summons and not an arrest warrant. Only if the official ignored the summons would a warrant for his arrest be issued. 18 PKPS 22 (Clause 2); 18 PKPS 175. By placing these preconditions upon suits involving government officials as defendants, it was apparently the king's intention to screen out frivolous suits which might interfere with the conduct of government business, even before the official himself ever had any notice that his behavior in office was under attack. The additional stipulation that a

summons rather than an arrest warrant should be issued may
have resulted from a desire to protect government officials
from the stigma of a criminal suit until their guilt was determined in a court of law.

A further limitation upon suits against government
officials was imposed by an order of the Minister of Justice
issued May 17, 1903. 19 PKPS 20. This order announced
that permission of the king must be obtained before directing
any criminal suits against officials who had been appointed
by the king himself. Such officials, for example, might
include military officers, judges, or commissioners whom
the king had appointed for work in the provinces. Permission
of the king was not required, however, for criminal suits
against officials appointed by ministers or ministry
officers. This limitation meant that the special status of the
king's own agents, those men operating with his special
authority in the affairs of government, would not be challenged
by the people except in matters which the king himself deemed
truly weighty and deserving of punishment. It cannot be doubted
that the requirement of royal approval must have acted as
a substantial deterrent to suits against the king's appointees.
This was true not only because of the hesitation of the common
people in approaching the king directly, but also because the
rule emphasized the special relationship between such officials
and the king, making it appear that any reproach directed against
the officials was in some measure a reproach against the king
himself. For this reason, the rule served to cloak the officials
whom the king himself had appointed with a special status and an
aura of inviolability which few must have dared to challenge.

Government officials during the reign of King Chulalongkorn
were subject to greater and more detailed regulation of their
behavior in office than had previously been the case. In the newly
restructured judiciary, private citizens could more readily enforce
these regulations when official misconduct occurred. Certain
limitations still restricted the bringing of such suits, some
designed to prevent frivolous suits from obstructing normal
government work and some designed to protect the special status
of officials who were the king's "own men." In neither instance
were such suits prohibited; but it became necessary that an extra
step be taken, that an extra burden of proof be satisfied, or that

the king's approval first be obtained. These restrictions were important but did not necessarily prevent valid suits from being brought, and their existence may in the long run be less remarkable than the expanded opportunities which the people had obtained to hold government officials accountable for their behavior in office.

C. The Right to Fair Treatment by the Judicial and Penal System

Probably the most dramatic gains in the rights of private citizens came in their dealings with the judiciary. The king himself, in his speech at the opening of the Legislative Council in 1895, had announced certain standards of judicial fair treatment which he wished to see enacted into law. He desired that the individual and his property be protected by laws which would apply in the same manner throughout the country. He desired not only that such laws be fair and merciful, but that they be clear and certain in their terms so that no confusion could exist as to what was prohibited and what was permitted. The king believed that the poor as well as the rich should have access to the court system, and that criminal defendants should be investigated and tried in a fair manner without unnecessary delay. This speech, coming on the eve of the most dramatic legal reforms of King Chula-longkorn's reign, announced certain norms of fairness and equality which would shape the legislation to be enacted during the king's final fifteen years. 14 PKPS 336.

The goal of uniformity, of equal application of all laws throughout the country, was pursued both in the geographical sense and in the social sense. Geographically, the judicial system was extended to nearly every region of the country and the laws were to be applied uniformly by judges under the centralized control of the Ministry of Justice. A notable exception, of course, was the small Muslim area along the southern border where an enclave of Islamic law still existed. Socially, the laws were applied equally to all subjects regardless of status, with certain exceptions in the case of royalty

and government officials. [11]   Social equality under law
represented a major change from the traditional legal theory.
The old system of punishment, for example, was theoretically
based on the sakdina of the parties involved. If a defendant with
high sakdina was found guilty under traditional law his punishment was more severe than for a defendant of lesser social
status because he had failed to behave in a manner appropriate
to his position. If a defendant with low sakdina committed a
crime against a person of high status, his punishment was
increased according to the sakdina of his victim. [12]   This
system was abandoned under King Chulalongkorn, and the
punishments specified under the new criminal laws were
applied in theory without regard to social rank.

The clarity and certainty of law desired by King
Chulalongkorn was attained in large measure by the
promulgation of extensive and detailed codes, both substantive
and procedural. To a degree never before seen in Thai legal
history, citizens were told precisely which acts were prohibited
by law and what legal defenses might be raised in various
criminal actions. They were told what sort of conduct would
constitute a cause of action for a civil suit. They were informed
in detail as to how a court might acquire jurisdiction over the
person or property of the defendant, and what types of cases
could be brought in the different courts. Judicial procedures
were set forth in detail, and the parties were warned as to which
actions would constitute contempt or an obstruction of justice.
The power of the court to render judgements was described in
detail, as was the right of the losing party to appeal those
judgements. In short, the king had effectively granted to the
people a right against arbitrary and capricious applications of
the law, against the taking of liberty or property without proper
notice as to the legal justification for such action by the state.
King Chulalongkorn had created a new legal standard requiring
that the law function in a predictable and foreseeable manner
in its regulation of the affairs of the people.

The right of the people to a fair trial was articulated
with some precision. In 1894 an extensive new law of evidence
and witnesses was enacted. In 1896 the Law of the Provincial
Courts clearly delineated the procedures to be followed in the
courts of the land and the powers which the various courts could

lawfully exercise. The code of civil procedure, and the provisional law of civil procedure before it, set forth the rules for bringing suit, for argument by the parties, and for the rendering of a decision by the court, as well as the proper method to follow for appeals. The Law of the Courts of Jusice of 1908 provided a further explanation of the manner in which all courts were expected to operate in order to ensure a fair trial. The proper procedure to be followed in trials for punishable offenses was set forth in provisional form in 1896 and was later to be enacted as a code of criminal procedure. In 1900 an important revision of the rules of evidence permitted either party to testify in his own behalf and to call his spouse, his children, or his relatives as witnesses. 17 PKPS 195 (Clause 6). The right of representation at trial by a qualified attorney was guaranteed in the provisional law of punishable offenses, 15 PKPS 106 (Section 9), and in the code of civil procedure, 22 PKPS 254 (Section 17). Through provisions such as these, a definition and a guarantee of fair trial emerged to protect all citizens who came into contact with the judicial system.

King Chulalongkorn had emphasized that criminal defendants were entitled to a speedy trial without unnecessary delay or detention. These rights were enacted into law through a series of statutes. Under the provisional law of punishable offenses of 1896, it was required that no suspect be arrested without a warrant unless caught in the commission of a crime or likely to escape before such a warrant could be obtained. The warrant had to specify in detail the crime of which there was reason to believe that the suspect was guilty. 15 PKPS 106 (Clause 1). In the Law of Provincial Administration of 1897, it was forbidden to imprison any person without evidence. No imprisonment was permitted, moreover, unless pursuant to a judicial decision, a suit by some plaintiff, a court order, or some cause to arrest the suspect. 16 PKPS 22 (Clause 45, Paragraph 2).

These laws protecting against detention without cause were supplemented by enactments providing for the

speedy trial of the accused. In a proclamation of July,
1884, it was observed that many officials failed to send
criminal suspects quickly to the proper court for trial.
This was considered unfair not only to innocent persons
wrongly detained, but to guilty persons as well who were
forced to suffer the additional hardship of a lengthy
detention without trial. To correct this unfairness, it
was ordered that all officials attempt to expedite the
trial of criminal defendants and to avoid improper delay.
10 PKPS 172. Later, under the provisional law of punishable offenses, it was required that, after arresting a
criminal suspect, the investigation of his case should not
last more than forty-eight hours unless some written
explanation were submitted to justify the delay. In addition,
judges were required to hand down their verdict within
three days of the trial's end. The defendant, if found to be
innocent, must be released at once without further imprisonment or prosecution. 15 PKPS 106 (Clauses 3, 20, 37).

In addition to these safeguards against arrest and
imprisonment without cause and unnecessarily protracted
periods of detention, there was also an attempt to prevent
coerced confessions of guilt both before and during trial.
In a royal edict of March 1, 1897, it was observed that
the traditional practice of the police was to torture criminal
defendants in order to extract confessions of their guilt.
The trial judge under traditional law could order that the
defendant be tortured to obtain a confession whenever the
court possessed evidence of the defendant's guilt, and the
defendant refused voluntarily to confess his wrongdoing.
The edict of 1897 criticised this practice both because it
might unintentionally be used against an innocent person
and because the evidence produced by such coercive
methods was inherently unreliable. Since the new rules
of criminal procedure and the new rules of evidence and
witnesses already provided a fast and reliable means to
find the truth in criminal cases, it was no longer necessary
to resort to torture of the defendant. For this reason,
the practice was banned and made punishable under law.
15 PKPS 243. The right of the defendant against
involuntary self-incrimination during the trial itself was

protected in a proclamation of February 19, 1900. 17 PKPS 195. This proclamation, which granted each of the parties the right to testify in his own behalf or to call the opposing party to testify, also provided that the plaintiff in a criminal case could never call the defendant to testify. In this way the criminal defendant was protected against the possibility that he would be forced to incriminate himself through his own testimony.

Another right associated with the trial process to which some attention was given was the right of an indigent party to a fair trial. In a proclamation of June 18, 1892, the right of poor people to bring suits in the courts of the Ministry of Justice was guaranteed, and all filing fees and court costs were to be waived in such cases. The indigent plaintiff was required to pay the court, however, if he obtained sufficient funds during the course of the trial or as a result of the court's judgement in the case. 13 PKPS 164. This proclamation was apparently misused a great deal by persons pretending to be indigents, however, and it was rescinded on March 29, 1893. At that time a new rule was enacted with a more detailed procedure for determining the financial status of the purportedly indigent plaintiff. Only after these procedures were satisfied could the judge grant the plaintiff's petition to waive all expenses. If, however, the plaintiff should lose or abandon his suit, the court was required to order full payment of the expenses which had been waived on account of indigency. This curious provision, which appears to squeeze blood from a stone, was perhaps based on the assumption that the plaintiff's family or relatives could be held liable for the payment of these fees. Again it was provided that the plaintiff be required to pay all costs in full if he should acquire sufficient funds in the course of the trial or as the result of a favorable verdict. 13 PKPS 172.

In the provisional law of civil procedure of 1896, both plaintiffs and defendants who lacked funds were permitted to argue their cases without payment of normal court costs. An oath of indigency was required, and a

penalty of six months imprisonment was to be imposed
upon the plaintiff, but apparently not the defendant, for
perjury in this regard. In all other respects, the law of
1893 appeared to remain intact. 15 PKPS 157 (Clauses
122-129). By a rule of the Ministry of Justice issued
January 23, 1903, however, compliance with the law on
indigent parties was strengthened by giving the defendant
an opportunity to disprove an assertion of indigency by the
plaintiff. His reward, should he succeed in proving that
the petition for indigent status was without merit, would
be an immediate dismissal of the entire suit. 18 PKPS
540. Provisions on indigent parties contained in the civil
procedure code of 1908 (Clauses 115-122) did not appear
to alter significantly the law existing at that time. 22
PKPS 254.

　　　　The concern for rights of impoverished parties
during trial was further evidence of a general attitude
that the judicial process should not be used in an abusive
or oppressive manner. A similar attitude led to the
enactment of laws dealing with matters which arose after
the verdict of the trial court. Appeals have been discussed
already in Chapter 3. They were now regarded as a matter
of right, at least at the first appellate level, and were no
longer treated as criminal suits against the trial judge.
The manner in which this right was to be exercised was
clearly described by the laws of civil and criminal procedure. Criminal defendants äfter conviction were also
protected to some extent from the cruelty of corporal
punishment. Although corporal punishment was not abandoned altogether, it was in 1896 replaced with imprisonment
for those crimes which were previously punishable by
fifty lashes or less. 15 PKPS 49.

　　　　Some attention was also given to the last stage of
the criminal process, the Thai prison system. In a
remarkable order issued probably in 1899 (undated),
rules for the regulation and inspection of provincial prisons
were set forth. The rights even of convicted criminals
were to some extent defined and protected. The provincial
governor was required to inspect the prisons at least once

every seven days, both during the daytime and at night.
(Paragraphs 2 and 3). He was required to do all in his
power to administer and improve the prisons. (Paragraph
5). He was ordered to meet with the prisoners and to
hear their complaints. (Paragraph 4). Inmates who were
addicted to drugs were to be treated by doctors and helped
to overcome their addiction. (Paragraph 36). Prison
officials were not allowed to beat inmates except to defend
themselves or others when attacked. (Paragraph 41).
Weapons were not to be used against the prisoners unless
they attacked prison officials by the use of greater force
or unless they attempted to escape. (Paragraph 42).
Regulations also controlled the work to be performed by
the inmates, clothing and other items which were to be
distributed, and punishments which might lawfully be
imposed for misbehavior by the inmates. It was required
that each new inmate be informed of all these regulations.
(Paragraph 83). 17 PKPS 148.

The order regarding provincial prisons is typical
of many of King Chulalongkorn's judicial enactments in its
broad scope, its particularity of detail, and its requirement
of fair treatment. To a degree never before achieved, the
rights of private citizens in their dealings with the judicial
and penal system were guaranteed under law. At each stage
in the trial process, as well as in pre-trial and post-trial
matters, standards of fairness were defined and made
enforceable against the officials involved. Whether or not
such standards were strictly observed and enforced at all
times, the conceptual foundations of the entire judicial
process had been radically altered. The judiciary was no
longer a powerful mechanism by which sacred laws were to
be applied arbitrarily to largely passive litigants. Instead
it had become an agency which, by means of detailed laws
and procedures, was to ascertain the truth and vindicate
the rights of the parties according to new standards of
fairness and propriety. By these standards the judges
were bound and could be held strictly accountable to
private citizens who had dealings with the judicial process.

D. Rights of Speech

The protection of free speech remained throughout
the legal reforms of King Chulalongkorn an area of some
uncertainty. In Chapter 2 the rights of speech accorded
to the king's legislative advisers were described, and a
basic ambivalence in the attitude of the king was noted.
Although he permitted and even encouraged free speech
and criticism among his legislative councilors, he also
wished to retain substantial control over the matters
which they discussed. There was no public aspect to the
rights of speech guaranteed the king's legislative advisers.
They met privately and their primary function was to keep
the king, not the public, informed and to assist him in
drafting and evaluating new laws. In the area of public
speech by ordinary citizens, the issue became even more
problematic and the apparent ambivalence grew even more
pronounced.

In some instances the legal limits imposed upon
speech were strict and clear. Speech criticizing judges
in the performance of their duty, for example, was sharply
limited. In the provisional law of civil procedure, any
utterance which was directed against judges or against any
court during the performance of their functions and was
found to be improper, could be punished by as much as
twelve months imprisonment or a one thousand baht fine or
both. 15 PKPS 157 (Clause 140). A similar proscription
was contained in the later civil procedure code enacted
in 1908. 22 PKPS 254 (Clause 136).

In other areas, however, the problem was a good
deal more complex. A royal ordinance promulgated in
April 1899 dealt directly with the difficult questions
involved in the law of defamation. 17 PKPS 14. This
ordinance began with a historical perspective. In the
reign of King Chulalongkorn's predecessor, according to
the ordinance, it was unclear whether defamation was a
punishable offense or not. King Mongkut had maintained
that no legal action was necessary when injurious

criticisms of the government or the people were published because everyone would know that such publications were false. If they were in fact true, then the speaker would have had no reason to publish them. His natural course of action would have been to bring such criticisms before a court of law or before the king himself. The fact that he had failed to do so indicated that his criticisms were without foundation and would be regarded as such by all who heard them. For this reason, according to King Mongkut, it was unnecessary for the government to take action against those who defamed it.

In the age of King Chulalongkorn, the ordinance explained, private citizens had gained more freedom and opportunity to disseminate views which were critical both of the government's operations and of individual government officials. While this was good in the sense that it permitted honest, well-intended expressions of feelings, it was bad in so far as it gave sanction to dishonest purposes, to the intentional destruction of reputation, and to deliberate attempts to obstruct progress in the country. For this reason, a new law of defamation was necessary, and the royal ordinance of 1899 set forth the new rules which were to be observed.

The first prohibition involved speech which might injure Thailand's relationship with foreign allies. Defamatory utterances directed against the leaders of foreign nations with whom Thailand had friendly relations were punishable even, it appears, if such utterances were truthful or not maliciously intended. If, however, such speech was permitted under the law of the country against which it was directed, then the Thai government would also refrain from punishment. (Clause 4). This exception was apparently abandoned in the criminal code of 1908 which dealt with crimes against diplomatic relations, and included provisions similar in all other important respects to the defamation ordinance of 1899. 22 PKPS 1 (Clause 113).

A second area of proscribed speech involved

criticism of the Thai government or king. It was generally forbidden under the ordinance of 1899 to encourage people to distrust the monarch, the existing methods of government under law, the Legislative Council or the actions of the judiciary; it was forbidden to encourage the people to change the form of government by extra-legal means; and it was forbidden to create animosity and dissent among the people. All of these actions were punishable offenses under law. It was possible, however, for a person accused of such crimes to raise as a defense the fact that he merely intended to point out a failure of the government to perform its duties properly. In asserting such a defense, the speaker had to show: (1) that he actually believed that his proposed changes in the government's method of operation would improve the existing situation; (2) that he intended to persuade the people to accomplish such changes by lawful means; and (3) that he intended to point out a governmental practice which he believed injurious in that it created animosities and dangerous conditions, and that his intent in pointing out such a practice was to change or abolish it. (Clause 5).

This legal defense to a charge of defamation was extremely significant in its implications as to the proper role of the people in seeking governmental reform. It would appear to protect speech which was directed toward such reform, so long as it was not maliciously motivated and did not advocate violation of the law. The defense was not provided in the provisions of the criminal code of 1908 which dealt with speech directed against members of the royal family and regents, however, and was probably not available in such cases. 22 PKPS 1 (Clauses 98, 100).

The right of free speech thus remained a problem-atic area under the laws of King Chulalongkorn's era. Only a year before the enactment of the royal ordinance on defamatory speech in April of 1899, a western newspaper publisher named J.J. Lilly[13] had been deported from Thailand for printing in his Bangkok newspaper and sending to European publishers certain articles critical of the Thai government. Mr. Lilly's error had been to imply in

his writings that the government was unable to protect
the persons and property of foreign visitors to Thailand.
16 PKPS 157.

The king seemed to believe that a balance had to
be struck between utterances which could help to bring
about constructive reforms of governmental practices
and utterances which might endanger Thailand's relations
with other countries or the security of her own domestic
institutions. The distinction was a difficult one.
Thailand's laws and institutions were undergoing such
radical changes that it could not have been clear to
many people which ideas might lawfully be advocated and
which ideas were too threatening to the existing government. A great deal of discretion thus remained in the
person of the king as to how strictly he wished to limit
public speech. The provisions of the royal ordinance of
1899 could have served as the basis for a great expansion
of the citizen's role in advocating governmental change,
for there was some indication that honest, well-intended
criticism was both necessary and desirable for the
effective administration of the country. But much would
depend on the wishes of the monarch himself. The
counter-interest of foreign relations and domestic security,
together with the inviolability of the monarchy itself,
could easily be asserted as necessary limitations on the
individual's rights of speech.

E. The Right to Representation in Government

Although the royal ordinance on defamatory speech
of 1899 implied that the people might exercise an
influential role in effecting governmental change, no
important political institution was created by which the
people could participate in the decisions of the central
government. Much of King Chulalongkorn's legislation
was enacted to improve the welfare of the people and to
abolish oppressive practices, but this legislation was
still created by unilateral royal mandate rather than

popular consensus. The people still had no direct role
either in the enactment of laws or in the administration
of the country. Legislators were not chosen by the
public, but were appointed and controlled strictly by
the king. The distribution of power was far different
from what it would become after 1932, when the power of
the people was declared supreme and Parliament, which
was considered the primary representative of the popular
will, was given a dominant voice in the workings of the
government.

During the reign of King Chulalongkorn, however,
the law did give citizens the right to choose their own
representatives in the two levels of the provincial
administration which were closest to the people. The
phu yai ban, or village headman, was to be chosen by the
men and women of his village in an election administered
by the district chief and held either publicly or privately
as the people should desire. The duties of the phu yai ban
were generally to care for the welfare of the villagers,
to investigate suspicious occurrences, and to mobilize the
villagers for activities such as catching criminals or
putting out fires. 16 PKPS 22 (Clauses 9, 12 of the Law
of Provincial Administration, May 20, 1897).

The head of the tambon government, an administrative unit consisting of approximately ten villages, was
elected by a meeting of all phu yai ban in that tambon.
This official, the kamnan, was jointly responsible with all
the phu yai ban for protecting the laws and the peace and
welfare of the villagers. He transmitted complaints of
the villagers to the provincial government and from the
provincial and central government he transmitted laws to
the villagers. The kamnan had the power to call the phu
yai ban together for meetings and to initiate proceedings
against any phu yai ban or villager who should disobey
his orders. In addition, the kamnan's duties were to
protect the order and harmony of the tambon, to assist
and inform the district government regarding criminal
matters arising in the tambon, to investigate suspicious
activities within the tambon, to aid in the collection of

taxes, and to help officials of the central government who travelled to his tambon. 16 PKPS 22 (Section 4).

The kamnan and the phu yai ban, chosen directly or indirectly by the people, played an important role in the administration of the day-to-day affairs of the villagers. Their authority was, however, sharply limited by the power of the district (amphoe) council, an appointed body which supervised their work and could expel them from office at least temporarily whenever they were found guilty of misconduct. Beyond the district level, of course, the power of the provincial and the regional governments, all non-elective bodies, was quite strong and was representative of the king rather than of the local populace. Nevertheless, the right to exercise a voice in the selection of the phu yai ban and the kamnan was an important one. The power of the king had been extended downward towards the people, and the power of the people had been extended upward as far as the tambon level. At least in theory, there was little room for the arbitrary and self-serving behavior of entrenched officials who represented neither the king nor the people. Moreover, the procedure of holding elections at the local level made the practice a familiar one to the people and could have served as preparation for elections on a larger scale in the future. In this sense the practice was significant not only for the present role it gave the people in the local administration of their own affairs, but for the future role it might portend in the affairs of the central government. The right to a representative government, once granted at the local level, could more easily be extended to the regional and national levels if future leaders should choose to embark upon that political course.

116

NOTES

1. Akin Rabibhadana, p. 99, points out that the
    fifth and sixth ranks -- mǫm ratchawong and mǫm
    luang -- were not, strictly speaking, considered
    to be čhao.

2. See Chapter 2, note 2.

3. Discussion of the four social groups appears in
    Akin Rabibhadana, pp. 98-112.

4. Akin Rabibhadana, pp. 179- 184.

5. The tax farming system is described in Walter
    F. Vella, Siam Under Rama III, 1824-1851
    (New York, 1957), p. 23.

6. These explanations are offered by Charern
    Chaichana in Sangkom süksa [Social Studies]
    (Bangkok, 1959), excerpted in Chulalongkorn the
    Great, Prachoom Chomchai, ed. and trans.
    (Tokyo, 1965), p. 60.

7. Prachoom Chomchai, pp. 56-58.

8. Phra Wǫraphakphibun, p. 106.

9. Phra Wǫraphakphibun, p. 118.

10. Akin Rabibhadana, p. 84.

11. Restrictions placed upon lawsuits directed against
    government officials and persons appointed by the
    king are discussed at pp.   above.

Residents of the royal palace were also given
special treatment by the Thai judicial system.
On June 8, 1895 jurisdiction over such persons
was withdrawn from the courts of the Ministry
of Justice and granted instead to the Palace
Ministry by Royal Letter (phraratchahatlekha)
No. 6. Later, however, jurisdiction of the
Palace Ministry was restricted to cases in
which (1) the defendant was a person not allowed
outside the royal palace, or (2) the cause of
action arose in the palace. Thanin Krawichian,
Kan patirup robop kotmai ..., p. 51.

12. Phra Wǫraphakphibun, p. 137. Another instance
of different treatment for different social classes
under the old legal system is cited by Constance
M. Wilson. She notes that, during the reign of
King Mongkut, ordinary courts were deprived of
any jurisdiction whatsoever over royalty, residents of the Inner Palace, and certain persons of
high status. Cases involving such persons were
decided instead by a special court or by a
specially designated arbiter. Constance M. Wilson,
"State and Society..." pp. 408-409.

13. The spelling of Mr. Lilly's name, transliterated
into English from Thai, may be inaccurate.

CHAPTER 5

CONCLUSION

The legal foundations of Thai kingship had undergone a profound shift during the reign of King Chulalongkorn.
Under traditional theory the Thai king had been the center
of the legal system. Sacred law, as embodied in the
thammasat, legitimated the king's rule, and the king in
turn legitimated the laws of the kingdom in his role as
protector and interpreter of the thammasat. The monarchy
was the center, the nucleus, the purpose of the government itself. By the time of King Chulalongkorn's death in
1910, however, the traditional theories of royal legitimacy
had been irrevocably changed. New laws had seemingly
created new legal rights, and the relationship between the
government and the people appeared to have undergone a
remarkable transformation.

The development in the theory of law and kingship
was, however, uneven and at times inconsistent. In
certain areas the written laws grew and changed with great
speed. This was particularly true of the judicial function
generally and of individual rights in relation to the justice
system. In other areas there was little change, or else
the changes were ambivalent or even regressive from the
later constitutional viewpoint. The legislative function,
for example, remained the prerogative of the king alone
and he, with the assistance of his legislative councils,
exercised this prerogative in a unilateral and vigorous
manner. Rights of free speech and of representation in
government remained ambiguous at best, dependent upon
future political events for their development and
clarification.

The prevailing theory of law and kingship, because

119

of its uneven rate of development, grew to contain certain contradictions which were all but irreconcilable. A broad spectrum of legal rights was granted to the people of the kingdom, and yet the people were given no role in enacting the legislation which created or modified such rights. Governmental decrees were enacted for the benefit and welfare of the people, and yet the entire legislative process remained in the hands of a small elite group. The people were given new remedies against judges and government officials who failed to administer the laws in a fair and proper way, and yet the people had no voice in the selection of those persons who ruled over them. Limitations were imposed upon the legitimate exercise of power by government officials, and yet the authority of the king remained absolute.

These conceptual contradictions may have had little real significance during a time when change and progress were already proceeding at an unprecedented speed. The retention of vast political power by the king, moreover, was surely welcomed by a public which held King Chulalongkorn in the highest esteem and regarded him as a uniquely wise and able ruler. As in the days of the paternalistic monarchy, the power of the king promoted and protected the welfare of the people rather than infringing upon their interests.

The laws enacted under King Chulalongkorn are not to be compared, however, with traditional legislation enacted under previous paternalistic Thai kings. There had occurred a fundamental change in the nature and the effect of the new laws, and this change was to have a profound significance in later years. The broad new legal structure created by King Chulalongkorn was more than rachasat, or temporary royal law subject to complete revision or nullification by succeeding monarchs in so far as it was found to depart from the teachings of Manu. Although these laws could in theory be taken away by the same absolute power which granted them, it is nearly impossible to imagine such a wholesale revocation occurring in practice. Particularly in the area of individual rights a certain legitimacy arose from the survival of these laws over time, from their continuing role in the courts of justice, and from the prestige and authority of the king who promulgated them. While they lacked the permanent quality of constitutional guarantees, they became to a certain degree inviolable in so far as they stated a new role for the private citizen in the conceptual framework of law and kingship. They were not mere rachasat in the traditional sense, whose existence was dependent upon the approval of future monarchs, for they represented a deeper and more fundamental change, a departure from the thammasat itself as the legitimizing principle for legislative enactments of the king.

Subsequent historical events proved that this was indeed the case. Rama VI and Rama VII made no attempt to nullify the body of law which King Chulalongkorn had created. Yet they both failed to pursue the logic of the reforms which had been enacted, to continue the developmental process which their predecessor had set in motion. The internal contradictions which may have seemed less important under King Chulalongkorn's rule now loomed larger. Unable to justify their absolute power by reference to the outmoded theory of traditional kingship, King Rama VI and Rama VII were also unwilling to continue the development of a coherent new system. They would not go forward in promoting the newer theories of law and government and they could not go backward in justifying their rule through traditional claims of royal legitimacy which had begun to appear unfair and outdated.

Certain concepts born in the reforms of King Chulalongkorn were taken up by the revolutionary movement of 1932 to justify opposition to the absolute rule of King Rama VII. A major point of dissatisfaction, for example, was the special status of the royal princes under King Rama VII. They were seen as a class above the laws and the jurisdictional authority of the Thai judiciary. Only with the permission of the king could a suit be brought against this group. The revolutionary leaders believed that the special status of the princes created an unjust system in which one class ruled over another class, the latter having no legal remedy for misconduct or impropriety on the part of their rulers.[1] This particular issue may be traced directly to the legal reforms of King Chulalongkorn. His enactments had seemed to create a new guarantee that all officials could be held accountable under law for their behavior in office. Moreover, the king himself had promoted the notion of equality under law for all persons regardless of social class. Nevertheless, King Chulalong- korn had also sought to protect certain officials from direct legal action without his consent, and had always insisted upon the inviolability of the royal institution itself. This apparent inconsistency, which was probably of little consequence during the reign of King Chulalongkorn, became a major political issue under his successors.

Similarly the area of free speech, which had remained ambiguous under King Chulalongkorn, became a source of political friction under the succeeding monarchs. Both Rama VI and Rama VII attempted to censor the press when it published political criticism by discontented Thai citizens or by foreigners residing in Thailand. [2] This restriction of the right of free speech, although clearly appropriate under the older theories of absolute rule, must have appeared inconsistent with the newer guarantees of individual rights under law. King Chulalongkorn himself had desired that the public participate constructively in criticizing and reforming the government. At the same time, however, he had left open the possibility that speech too threatening to the existing government would be punishable under law. Once again, an ambiguity in the earlier period grew into a genuine political issue in the later period when succeeding rulers failed to acknowledge the force of the newer legal theories.

An announcement by the revolutionary People's Party explained to the people of Thailand in 1932 why it had become necessary to overthrow the monarchy:

> When the present king [Rama VII] came
> to the throne the people hoped that he would
> give an equitable administration. Their
> hopes were unfulfilled. The king was above
> the law even as his predecessors had been.
> His relatives and friends, even when without
> ability, were given the highest government
> positions. The king allowed government officials
> to be dishonest. They took personal graft in
> governmental building projects, in buying
> supplies, and in the exchange of government

money. The king elevated the royal class and
permitted them to oppress the common people.
The king ruled unwisely and allowed the country
to fall into decay, as the present depression
proves. The government of the king, who is
above all law, is unable to right these wrongs. [3]

Traditionally there had been no doubt that the king was "above all
law" in the sense that he alone could translate the precepts of the
thammasat into specific rules of conduct by which his subjects were
to be bound. The king himself was ruled only by the generalized
moral obligations listed in the thammasat as kingly virtues or as
principles of justice. By 1932, however, many believed that the
rule of law was superior to the power of kingship itself, that the
laws existed apart from the king and that the people possessed
certain rights which even the king could not disregard. This newer
theory of law and kingship, while owing much to the influence of
European political philosophy, may also be traced to the dramatic
expansion of individual rights under King Chulalongkorn, to the new
rules of judicial due process, and to the suggestion that all persons
should be governed equally by the laws of the kingdom.

This is not to say that the revolution was caused
directly by theoretical inconsistencies originating in the reforms
of King Chulalongkorn. Other factors, commonly cited by historians,
undoubtedly produced the revolution in the immediate sense. There
was, for example, the influence of European education upon the
movement's leaders, the effects of the economic depression, the
dismissal by King Rama VII of large numbers of salaried government officials, and the demand of a growing educated class for a
role in the administration of the government. Many observers have
stressed the sometimes arbitrary behavior of King Rama VI and
King Rama VII, together with the latter's lack of political experience.
It is often said that King Rama VII was unprepared for the task of
governing and was too dependent upon the advice of the royal princes,
who tended to promote their own interests over those of other
officials and of the public.

Moreover, the revolution itself should not be interpreted
as a broadly based movement of the Thai people attempting to secure
certain rights which they themselves had come to consider essential.
The revolution, like the reforms of King Chulalongkorn, was

primarily a change from above, a transformation brought about by a relatively small and elite group. Although its object may have been the vindication of certain rights of the people, its beginnings are not to be found in the public at large. The new theories of individual rights under law had not yet become revolutionary instruments in the hands of the Thai people generally.

In a broader sense, however, a causal chain may be traced from the reforms of King Chulalongkorn to the revolution of 1932. The transformation of laws and government by King Chulalongkorn created a disequilibrium in the concept of monarchical rule, an implicit set of contradictions with regard to the king and his relationship to the law. Subsequent events changed these conceptual inconsistencies into issues of real political discontent, issues which could no longer be confined within the bounds of absolute kingship.

There was a strong inner logic to the new theories which King Chulalongkorn had enacted into law. This logic demanded that the theories not be accepted piecemeal. They could not exist harmoniously with the older theories which they tended to displace. The concepts of equality under law, of commonly-held individual rights, of government for and -- to some extent -- by the people, once set in motion could not easily be contained. Inevitably the newer theories tended to clash with the older theories, to create crucial points of weakness in the conceptual framework of law and kingship. In the later period of political strain and economic and administrative difficulties, the framework was to collapse at precisely those points.

NOTES

1. Luang Vichitr Vadhakarn stressed this issue in Kan
    müang kan pokkhrǫng khǫng krung sayam (Bangkok,
    1932), as quoted in Kenneth Perry Landon, Siam in
    Transition (Chicago, 1939), pp. 18-19.

2. See Vella, Impact of the West ..., pp. 361-362.

3. Quoted in Landon, p. 11.

BIBLIOGRAPHY

1. In Thai Language

Chompunut Nakiraks, "Bot bat khọng thi prüksa chao tang prathet
nai ratchasamai phrabat somdet phra čhunlačhọmklao
čhaoyuhua p. s. 2411- p. s. 2453 [The Role of Foreign
Advisers During the Reign of Rama V from 1868-1910],"
M. A. thesis, Chulalongkorn University, Bangkok, 1970.

Chulalongkorn, King, Phraratchadamrat song thalaeng phrabọrom-
marachathibai kaekhai kanpokkhrọng phaendin [Speech
Explaining the Governmental Reforms] . Bangkok, 1927.

------, Phraratchadamrat tọp khwamhen khọng phu čha hai plian
kan pokkhrọng [King Chulalongkorn's Reply to the
Opinioṇs of Those Who Would Change the Administration] .
From Čhaonai lae kharatchakan krap bangkhom thun
khwamhen čhat kanplianplaeng ratchakan phaendin r. s.
103 [Opinions on Instituting Governmental Change
Presented to the King in 1885] , pp. 51-60. Bangkok, 1967.

Damrong Rachanuphap, Prince, Laksana kan pokkhrọng prathet
sayam tae boran [The Administration of Siam from
Ancient Times]. Bangkok, 1933.

Kasem Sirisumpundh and Neon Snidvongs, "Naew phraratchadamri
thang kan müang nai phrabat somdet phra čhunlačhọmklao
čhaoyuhua [Political Thought of King Chulalongkorn] ,"
Sangkhomsat Parithat, 5, no. 3 (December 1967),pp. 25-46.

Phitchit Prichakọn, Prince, "Thammasan winitchai [A Consideration of Justice] ," in Prachum phraniphon krommaluang
Phitchit Prichakọn. Bangkok, 1929.

128

Sathian Laiyalak et al., comps., Prachum kotmai pracham sok
[Collected Laws, Arranged Chronologically] .
69 vols. Bangkok, 1935-53.

Thailand, Fine Arts Dept., comp., Chaonai lae kharatchakan krap
bangkhom thun khwamhen chat kanpliamplaeng ratchakan
phaendin r.s. 103 [Opinions on Instituting Governmental
Change Presented to the King in 1885] . Bangkok, 1972.

Thanin Kraiwichian, Kan patirup robop kotmai lae kan san nai
ratchasamai phrabatsomdet phrachunlachomklao
chaoyuhua phrapiyamaharat [Transformation of the
Legal System and the Judiciary During the Reign of
King Chulalongkorn] . Bangkok, 1968.

Woraphakphibun, Phra, Prawatsat kotmai thai [History of
Thai Law] . Bangkok, 1969.

2.   In English Language

Akin Rabibhadana, The Organization of Thai Society in the Early
Bangkok Period, 1782-1873. Ithaca, 1969

Coedès, G., The Making of South East Asia, trans. H.M. Wright.
Berkeley, 1969.

Darling, Frank C., "The Evolution of Law in Thailand,"
Review of Politics, 32, no. 2 (April 1970), pp. 197-218.

de Saint-Hubert, Christian, "Rolin-Jacquemyns (Chao Phya Aphay
Raja) and the Belgian Legal Advisers in Siam at the Turn
of the Century," Siam Society Journal, 53, pt.2 (Bangkok
1965), pp. 181-190.

Dhani Nivat, Prince, "The Old Siamese Conception of the
Monarchy," The Siam Society Fiftieth Anniversary
Commemorative Publication, 2 (Bangkok 1954), pp. 160-
175.

-------, "The Reconstruction of Rama I of the Chakri Dynasty,"
Selected Articles from the Siam Society Journal, 4
(Bangkok 1959), pp. 238-265.

Direck Jayanama, The Evolution of Thai Laws. Royal Thai
Embassy. Bonn, 1964.

Griswold, A.B. and Prasert na Nagara, "The Inscription of King
Rāma Gamhèn of Sukhodaya (1292 A.D.): Epigraphical
and Historical Studies No. 9," Siam Society Journal,
59, pt.2 (1971), pp. 179-228.

Hanks, Lucien M., "Merit and Power in the Thai Social Order,"
American Anthropologist, 64, no.6 (December 1962),
pp. 1247-1261.

Heine-Geldern, Robert, Conceptions of State and Kingship in
Southeast Asia. Ithaca, 1956.

Kasem Sirisumpundh, "Emergence of the Modern National
State in Burma and Thailand," Ph.D. diss., University
of Wisconsin, 1962.

Kemp, Jeremy, Aspects of Siamese Kingship in the Seventeenth
Century. Bangkok, 1969.

Landon, Kenneth Perry, Siam in Transition. Chicago, 1939.

Lingat, Robert, The Classical Law of India, trans. and additions
by J. Duncan M. Derrett. Berkeley and Los Angeles,
1973.

------, "Evolution of the Conception of Law in Burma and Siam,"
Siam Society Journal, 38, pt.1 (Bangkok 1959), pp. 9-31.

Masao, Tokichi, "The New Penal Code of Siam," 18 Yale Law
Journal 85 (December, 1908).

------, "The Sources of Ancient Siamese Law," 15 Yale Law
Journal 28 (November, 1905).

130

McLennan, Barbara N., "Concepts of Representation in Southeast Asia," Ph. D. diss., University of Wisconsin, 1965.

Parish, H. Carroll, "The Development of Democratic Institutions in Thailand," Ph. D. diss., University of California in Los Angeles, 1958.

Prachoom Chomchai, ed. and trans., Chulalongkorn the Great. Tokyo, 1965.

Sarasas, Phra, My Country Thailand. Bangkok, 1960.

Seni Pramoj, M. R., "King Mongkut as a Legislator," Selected Articles from the Siam Society Journal, 4 (Bangkok 1959), pp. 203-237.

Siffin, William, The Thai Bureaucracy. Honolulu, 1966.

Steinberg, David Joel, ed., et al., In Search of Southeast Asia. New York, 1971.

Vella, Walter F., The Impact of the West on Government in Thailand. Berkeley, 1955.

------, Siam Under Rama III, 1824-1851. New York, 1957.

Wales, H. G. Quaritch, Ancient Siamese Government and Administration. New York, 1965.

------, Siamese State Ceremonies. London, 1931.

Wenk, Klaus, The Restoration of Thailand under Rama I, 1782-1809, trans. Greeley Stahl. Tucson, Arizona 1968.

Wilson, Constance M., "State and Society in the Reign of Mongkut, 1851-1868: Thailand on the Eve of Modernization," Ph. D. diss., Cornell University, 1970.

Wilson, David A., Politics in Thailand. Ithaca, 1966.

Wyatt, David K., "Family Politics in Nineteenth Century
    Thailand," Journal of Southeast Asian History, 9,
    pt. 2, (1968), pp. 208-228.

------, The Politics of Reform in Thailand. New Haven, 1969.

THE UNIVERSITY OF MICHIGAN

CENTER FOR SOUTH AND SOUTHEAST ASIAN STUDIES

PUBLICATIONS

MP 3   Norman G. Owen, ed. Compadre Colonialism: Studies
on the Philippines under American Rule. Illustration, tables,
bibliography. 318 pp., paper.

MP 4   Frank Shulman. Doctoral Dissertations on South Asia,
1966-70. Appendices, indexes. xvii, 228 pp., paper.

MP 5   Harley Harris Bartlett. The Labors of the Datoe and
Other Essays on the Bataks of Asahan (North Sumatra).
Illustrations. xxiv, 387 pp., paper.

MP 6   John Stephen Lansing. Evil in the Morning of the World:
Phenomenological Approaches to a Balinese Community.
Illustration, bibliography. x, 104 pp., paper.

MP 7   Thomas R. Trautmann, ed. Kinship and History in South
Asia. Diagrams. ix, 157 pp., paper.

MP 8   William P. Malm and Amin Sweeney. Studies in Malaysian
Oral and Music Traditions. Illustrations. x, 104 pp., paper.

MP 9   David M. Engel. Law and Kingship in Thailand during
the Reign of King Chulalongkorn. Bibliography. 131 pp., paper.

MP 10   Thomas Poffenberger. Fertility and Family Life in an
Indian Village. Tables. 108 pp., paper.

Sp 1   Thomas Powers. Balita Mula Maynila (News from Manila).
Illustrations. 40 pp., paper.

LL 1   Peter Edwin Hook. The Compound Verb in Hindi. Index,
bibliography. 318 pp., paper.

For a current listing, please write:

CSSEAS Publications
130 Lane Hall
The University of Michigan
Ann Arbor, Michigan 48104

Printed and bound by CPI Group (UK) Ltd, Croydon, CR0 4YY

13/04/2025